Indispensable

About the Author

Chris Hirst is a leading authority on leadership and career success, and the award-winning author of *No Bullsh*t Leadership* and *No Bullsh*t Change*. Formerly Global CEO of Havas Creative, a multidisciplinary marketing services group, he built his career fixing broken businesses and leading high-performance teams around the world.

Chris is an Engineering Sciences graduate whose career began on the shop floor of a glass factory before taking him to the boardroom via Harvard Business School. He was named in the *Evening Standard* Power 1000, is regularly ranked as one of the marketing industry's most influential CEOs, and is a frequent commentator for BBC News, *Financial Times*, CNBC, Sky News and many more. *Indispensable* is his third book.

Find him on LinkedIn: @chris-hirst
www.chris-hirst.com

Indispensable

The No Bullsh*t Guide to Thriving At Work

CHRIS HIRST

MACMILLAN
BUSINESS

First published in the UK 2025 by Macmillan Business
an imprint of Pan Macmillan
The Smithson, 6 Briset Street, London ECIM 5NR
EU representative: Macmillan Publishers Ireland Ltd, 1st Floor,
The Liffey Trust Centre, 117–126 Sheriff Street Upper,
Dublin 1 DO1 YC43
Associated companies throughout the world

ISBN 978-1-5290-5174-2 HB
ISBN 978-1-5290-5175-9 TPB

3 5 7 9 8 6 4 2

A CIP catalogue record for this book is available from the British Library.

Typeset in Adobe Caslon Pro by Palimpsest Book Production Ltd, Falkirk, Stirlingshire
Printed and bound in India by Thomson Press India Ltd.

To Fred,
who slept under my desk throughout

Contents

Introduction

This book is a paean to careers: how to succeed at them, how to enjoy them, and, most important of all, how to make your career work for you.

There are those who consider work not as a worthy and rewarding way of spending our time, but at best as a necessary evil. Or even perhaps, an unnecessary evil, something imposed upon us, at odds with the natural order of mankind.

One of the arguments made by the work-as-tyranny camp is that a career is a chore rather than a vocation; that if your job is not your passion, how can it be anything but an imposition. This argument is wrong, impractical and disempowering. What if you cannot readily describe your passion, or are yet to uncover it? Where do you learn the skills, gain the confidence and find the contacts to pursue your dream? What if you have a mortgage to pay? And what do you do in the meantime, simply tread water hoping for inspiration?

My belief is that a successful career can be an end in itself as well as a means to an end. It can be a route to personal and financial reward, learning, fulfilment and future opportunity. However, it is an unavoidable fact that this is not the experience that many people have. The ambition of this book is to make sure one of those people is not you.

Through many years – from the shopfloor of a glass factory to CEO of a billion-dollar multinational; from a scrappy start-up to super-tanker corporate – I have done jobs I've loved and jobs I've hated. Periods where I felt I had the world at my feet and years when every step seemed to take me backwards and down. It is the way even the most successful careers go. However, in each case the primary determinant of my satisfaction and happiness was mostly unrelated to the 'what' of my role, but rather my sense of direction, the extent to which I felt I was moving forward and, of course, the people I worked with.

I can see now that I learned most when things were at their toughest. It's no consolation in the moment, of course, and failure only helps if we learn from it, but if we do it is a powerful engine for personal growth. The more successful somebody is, the more they have failed along the way; it's what we do with it that counts.

In time (and after a particularly grim period) I promised myself that I would no longer allow circumstance to control me, but that I would learn how to take control of my career – and stay in control even when the seas were at their most stormy.

Now the experiences, cultures and colleagues that both helped and hindered me form the foundations for this book. My hope is that the periods of happy progress, stumbling missteps and failures that make up my career can help inform yours. The principles I lay out are the foundation stones to all successful careers and apply to everybody who wishes to make the most of theirs.

I believe that human beings possess the innate desire to work, and to use work as a means to shape and develop their lives, even if for many it falls short of that ambition. I understand and empathise with the many people who experience work simply as a series of tasks that must be endured until they're allowed to go home.

But even if that is your experience, it is not inevitable nor impossible to change. A different career future is possible.

I've learned from experience that the people who succeed, who grow rich, who start successful companies, are no different to you and me. The skills you need to take control over your career demand clarity, will and practice to master, but none require any innate ability. You can do them all and I'm going to show you how – and in doing so help you take control over the direction and progress of your career.

Ultimately, it is how we work as much as what we do that determines our feelings towards our jobs. I have met numerous people in careers that many would consider to be dream jobs who have spent years being unhappy, stressed and deeply unfulfilled. These include the CEOs of major corporations, music industry executives on first-name terms with some of the world's biggest stars, hyper-remunerated fund managers, television producers, senior executives at the country's largest football clubs, airline pilots and many more. This is not to smash your dreams, but rather to point out that much of what makes work rewarding and enjoyable is how we do it, why we do it and the extent to which we feel it is helping us progress towards our personal goals, not just what we do. We want fulfilment, purpose, companionship and progress – as well as pay. However, simply waiting in the hope that those things will arrive unbidden is not a reliable strategy.

We must liberate ourselves to think clearly about what we want to get from our career – and accept that this is likely to change over time. What new experiences do we want it to provide, what do we wish to learn, how important to us are money, profile, autonomy, learning, position and power? Are we purpose-driven, goal-oriented or ambitious; what working patterns do we want?

A successful career is one that works for you, but it won't come without clarity, action and effort; it cannot simply be wished into existence. Careers are delicate truffles that must be assiduously rooted out, and to do that you'll need a map, compass and plenty of determination. The first two I hope to provide. The rest, as always, is up to you.

Through my career, I have come to the conclusion that leadership is the most powerful and useful skill we can learn – one that accelerates our progress, enables us to control our direction and lift others; when it comes to career success, it is not part of the game, it is the game. And it is a skill, as we will discover, that we can all learn. Yet too many of us are hobbled throughout our careers by ineffective leadership – leaders unable to offer us the purpose and supported autonomy that the human condition desires. Real-world experience quickly teaches us that it is perilous to rely solely on those we work for to take care of our careers and ambitions. Of course, sometimes we're lucky, we find a boss or an organisation able to lift us up, give us the skills and inspiration to reach higher than we might otherwise have done – perhaps higher than we ever dreamed. But too often that is not the case. Too many are leaders in title only.

One of the surest indicators of future career success is whether or not your first boss was themselves a high performer: great leaders beget great careers. But what if the person you work for isn't? If your boss can't run a meeting, who do you learn from? Where are you to turn for advice, support and useful feedback?

This, then, is the book you'll wish your boss had read; my ambition to provide you with a toolkit of skills that will make you indispensable, irrespective of position, ambition or role. I want to help you disconnect the rate at which you learn and progress from those you work with and for. If you want a better job, I have a plan to help. If you want to inspire your team to achieve more, I have a plan to help. If you feel like work just isn't working for you, I have a plan to help.

So ubiquitous are the foundational tasks, occupations and skills that make up the working day that they're barely discussed, never mind effectively taught. Yet they shape the rhythms of our working lives. From presentations and meetings to teams and culture, so much of how work works is taken for granted, done badly or simply ignored. The opportunity is not simply to do your job better – it is far greater. The principles laid out here present, for anybody who takes the time and care to do them well, a huge opportunity to stand out from the crowd, gain meaningful competitive advantage and so achieve their own ambitions. Not least because so many don't.

None are complicated; none are foolproof. But tear them out, take them with you, try them out and learn from where they lead you. They may not be what you expect, but they work. There's even a chapter about what to do if it's not working out – which is relevant to everybody, because sometimes it won't.

Indispensable people are those that organisations, clients, customers and teams feel they cannot lose without suffering loss themselves. This isn't a crazy dream; I have worked with many people like this, and it can be you too. The more valuable you become, the more opportunity you have, and ultimately opportunity is the path that leads to career freedom.

In a seminal study entitled 'The Mundanity of Excellence', Hamilton College's Professor Daniel Chambliss described talent as the consistent repetition of multiple mundane actions. Though work need not be mundane, much of what makes for excellent careers can be considered in a similar way: the development of skills and experience through the repetition of relatively uncomplicated tasks.

The intention of this book is to dispense with fine words and well-meaning platitudes; to help you understand what the person who hired you wants from you; to enable you to take control of your own career and in turn be brilliant for the careers of those you hire.

A career shouldn't be something that simply happens to us – it should be something we own and control.

So, without further ado, let's get started.

CHAPTER 1

Let Me Take Care of That

Over the past fifteen years, I have been responsible for over a hundred different companies across every continent, and worked with many more in sectors ranging from media and technology to packaged goods and financial services; from start-ups to multinationals. At first glance, they all appear to be completely different: the things they make, who they sell to, the way they describe themselves, their business models, the ways they make money. However, it has gradually become apparent to me that their differences are little more than skin deep; that despite outward appearances, the majority of what makes up a company's DNA is held in common with all others, irrespective of sector, size or market; that all companies are essentially the same. Their outward dressing obscures the commonalities which lie beneath.

Perhaps this should come as no surprise. All organisations are in essence simply collections of people trying to do a relatively common thing better than their competitors. They are all populated by people like you and me, people with the same ambitions, concerns and worries. When you talk to the people inside their walls, from the CEO to the receptionist, you hear the same questions and petty irritations everywhere.

This is because the largest and most important part of our jobs is dealing with other people – and people are all the same. If you ask a Chief Financial Officer (CFO) about the primary challenges they face, they will tell you about how the decisions and actions of their colleagues, customers or clients affect the numbers. In fact, many CFOs I have worked with talk of little else, usually in rather agricultural terms.

Career success is always determined by the same two factors, whether you work at Quantas or GSK, Alphabet or the Boston Public Library. They are aptitude and attitude. And though employers make a great fuss about required skills and experience on job descriptions when deciding who to hire or promote (aptitude), it is almost never the case that there is a uniquely qualified candidate. In fact, for many jobs there are usually a great many equally qualified candidates.

This might not be welcome news if you have spent many years building up your professional qualifications, but I'm sorry to say it's true. Experience, skills and qualifications might get you an interview, but will not get you the job. What gets you the job or the promotion, and indeed determines the entire course of your career, is attitude.

This is somewhat counter-intuitive, but very important to understand. The functional aspects of most jobs are not very difficult and can be rapidly learned. Even those that require a very high degree of skill quickly become mundane. For nearly everybody on the planet, transporting hundreds of people across the Atlantic in a heavier-than-air steel tube is unimaginable, but for an airline pilot it's just a job. Everything is difficult. Until it becomes easy.

It's not that skills don't matter. They matter very much. But they are very rarely the primary determinant of career success.

Aptitude and attitude

From our first job to our last, aptitude and attitude will determine our rate of progress – unless your mum or dad own the company. This is how prospective employers evaluate us, how decisions about promotions and pay rises are made and, in tough times, it's how redundancy processes are run.

Our net employability and future potential is the product of our aptitude and attitude. This might seem glaringly obvious, but it is easy to forget – as evidenced by many of those you see around you at work every day. When it comes to career potential, we could perhaps consider the relationship between the two as follows:

Career Potential = Attitude x Aptitude

It is a simple principle. Score low on either and, irrespective of how good we are at the other, it will significantly constrain our progress. Score well at both and the sky's the limit.

By way of example, let's consider high-jeopardy, high-skill roles, such as surgeons or airline pilots. High aptitude is of course a prerequisite, but attitude also matters. In *The Checklist Manifesto*, American surgeon and public health researcher Atul Gawande found that time and again in roles such as these, attitude matters a great deal, perhaps even above all. An example he returns to several times is where high-status, senior individuals are unwilling to take suggestions and advice from those they consider beneath them. Sound familiar? Gawande describes the sometimes fatal consequences of such behaviours in operating theatres and aeroplane cockpits.

If the right blend matters when our lives are at stake, I guarantee it matters if you wish to get hired, promoted and thrive anywhere else.

You will, of course, come across people who appear to be exceptions – those who do very well for themselves with little aptitude, a poor attitude, or both. This is the person with the right contacts, the right language and the right tie, who climbs all over everybody else to get the top job, who believes the rules don't apply to them. I cannot claim this doesn't happen because it demonstrably does. However, this success always comes at the expense of not just other individuals, but the collective team or organisation's performance.

Over many years, across the companies I have run, I've spent a considerable amount of time winkling such people out. Not just because it's the right thing to do (and is always popular with everybody else), but because, though they managed to advance themselves, they held the company and their colleagues back. Smart companies see through the bullshit to the charlatan beneath. Dumb ones – and I've worked for those too – don't.

The eight characteristics of the most successful people

As you progress through your career, aptitude will become increasingly specific to the experience you have gained and the skills you develop will tend to determine the sectors you can hope to work in. This is not to say you cannot change careers: some skills are transferable; new ones can be learned. However, the factor that always determines your rate of progress is attitude, irrespective of your position and career choice.

Because the DNA of all companies is very similar, it stands to reason that many of the attributes employers look for are the same across industries, both public and private. Employers want people who are going to rapidly become effective, productive and positive members of their team, which is what we also want for ourselves.

I'm not going to attempt to define an idealised individual. Not only is this impossible, it is undesirable. Nevertheless, who wouldn't want to work with somebody who was authentic, honest, supportive, generous of spirit, hard-working and able to make us smile when the going gets tough? None of us can be that person all the time, but all of us can be that person some of the time.

Here are the eight characteristics the most successful people I have worked with all share. And you can adopt them all with relative ease. I have spent a little more time expanding on the first two, because they are by far the most important and most commonly overlooked.

1. Be the person who gets sh*t done

There is no single thing that will more reliably make you indispensable in any role than having a reputation for getting things done.

It is both as simple and as difficult as that.

Many people believe that success at work is determined by intelligence and the ability to come up with great ideas, that this is where they can add greatest value. They become frustrated, even perhaps insulted, when their ideas are not acted upon or appear to be ignored. This is particularly the case with highly qualified graduates. But ideas are easy, ten-a-penny. Even strategy is not that difficult.

It's not that your employer doesn't want your ideas: they don't want any more ideas from anybody. They already have too many. What they need is people prepared to take them and make them happen. People who get shit done.

You will notice throughout your career that, when the heavy lifting is needed, the same people seem to drift away into the undergrowth. Yet at the end of the day, it's only getting stuff done that counts. Everything else is just thinking and talking.

Consequently, there are few statements more guaranteed to cement your role in any team than this one:

Let me take care of that.

People who take care of the boring, the mundane, the awkward, the difficult and the unglamorous are of an almost inestimable value – not least because of their relative scarcity. The person who takes tasks from you unbidden and completes them in a prompt and unfussy way demonstrates the single most desirable characteristic of a direct report in any industry and in any circumstance.

Do this and you'll always be asked back to any team. And the best thing of all is that you'll immediately stand out, because so many people spend so much time trying to do the opposite. They find all sorts of reasons to be somewhere else: they're too busy, it's not their job, they don't know how, why should they. It's beneath them.

Then they complain when you get the raise.

Organisations don't move in great leaps, but rather in multiple small steps. The nature of their progress is more akin to the rippling legs of a millipede than the bounds of a cheetah. Much that needs to be done is distinctly unglamorous, but somebody has to do it or nothing will happen.

People who show up every day and get shit done are worth their weight in gold. If there is one thing so many people fail to understand about their careers it is this.

If that is you, people will always want you around.

2. Bring solutions not problems

As humans, we're great at being able to point out all the things that are wrong, things that don't work properly and things others could do better. Perhaps this is evolutionary – recognising threats helped us stay alive. It can be useful at work too – up to a point. The problem is, because we're all good at it, a characteristic of many cultures becomes complaining; endlessly pointing out all the things that are wrong.

Your team may well have several people who specialise in this. Some mistake this for a sign of intelligence. It's not. It's easy, and unless it's accompanied by practical solutions, often unhelpful.

How do you feel around those people? How often do they say anything genuinely useful? Getting things done is hard work and naysayers don't simply suck energy from a room – they complicate, delay and derail. Don't be that person.

I have been responsible for running many successful change programmes. The identification of the principal challenges the organisation faces is a necessary first step; if you don't understand the problem, you can't fix it. However, this is generally neither difficult, nor new information. I found that people typically agreed that change was needed, but concluded the solution was for everybody else to raise their game. The same is found with day-to-day office complainers – the problem is always somebody else, never them.

In reality, change only happens when individuals are persuaded of the opposite, to stop complaining about everybody else and to think only of what they themselves will do differently.

I spent much of my career in advertising, where the creation and production of ideas was our business. I would watch nervous creatives present their scripts to the all-powerful creative director – a vulnerable and intimidating moment. I found it very easy to immediately see all that was wrong with an idea: it was too obtuse, or expensive, or derivative, or had the wrong tone. I clearly remember being shown a script that I thought so astonishingly odd I couldn't formulate a useful response at all, other than attempt to have it thrown out. It became one of the most successful adverts of all time.

Therefore, being a creative director is a difficult job. It is a position many attain, but few master. Those few, however, possess a remarkable clarity of thought and expression, coupled with the ability to be honest, insightful and constructive. I would watch (mostly in silence – I know my limits) as problems with an idea were identified, but also as advice was offered to the teams as to how they might be solved. All done under pressure, in public and instantaneously. The subjectivity of creativity makes it a remarkable and rare skill. A good creative director lifts all boats and helps everybody do better. Finding solutions, and helping others do the same, is difficult. But it's what business and successful careers are all about.

When you encounter problems, always think through potential solutions before you go and talk to somebody else. They may not agree with your recommendations, but it will make a world of difference to how they perceive you and how quickly solutions can be found. And remember that in business problem-solving means sweating the small stuff as well as the big. It's mostly the cumulative effect of solving lots of tiny issues that's significant.

Getting stuff done isn't standing at the back pointing to where the leaks are. It's wading into the freezing water with the gypsum, canvas and good humour to set about fixing them.

All teams love problem-solvers. They always get asked back.

3. Work hard

There is no path to success that does not involve hard work. Hard work is often confused with being busy. The two are not the same.

Productive work is the ability to focus your time on the most important tasks and reliably achieve them. This may not always require all of your time, but it will on occasion require a large amount of your energy – your most valuable resource.

Working hard is not the same as over-working. We will consider the implications of stress and burnout in a later chapter, but working hard should not mean working unhealthily. In order to be consistently productive, we need to be serious and deliberate about finding time and energy for all the other aspects of our lives – whether that be friends, family, hobbies or just sleep. This is how we recharge.

We must also ensure that those who work for us do the same. Not only are we responsible for their health and well-being at work, but taking that responsibility seriously is enlightened self-interest. If they thrive, you are more likely to succeed. If they fail, so might you.

Everybody has the same number of hours in their day and, when it comes to career success, focused hard work pays. There isn't a path to success without it – and don't believe the snake-oil salesmen who tell you otherwise.

4. Don't let fear of failure stop you from trying

I once interviewed Anthony Scaramucci for my podcast. He was (infamously) the White House Press Secretary for eleven days during Donald Trump's first term as President, before being publicly and humiliatingly fired. Scaramucci is a very successful and unexpectedly inspiring man, his career journey taking him from a blue-collar upbringing to Harvard, McKinsey and the cover of *Time* magazine. He freely admits he was 'exponentially naïve' in taking the White House job and is disarmingly honest about the pain of his ejection.

'Do you ever suffer from self-doubt?' I asked him.

He assured me he did. 'But here's the thing, Chris,' he continued. 'I don't let it stop me.'

It's true of all the most successful people I have ever met. They dislike, even fear failure as much as the rest of us. They too feel its pain. But the difference is, they don't let it stop them.

It is tempting, even comforting, to tell ourselves that successful people have been lucky and that everything has just gone their way. The opposite is true. I believe that successful people fail more than the rest of us, but in their failures lie their success.

5. Learn fast

The best people I have worked with may not let fear of failure hold them back, but that's because they learn very fast. I have been in teams with people who grew like sunflowers in the sun – you could almost see them change.

This isn't by accident. It is deliberate.

I imagine such people as being like children learning a language. Children learn languages quickly because they aren't worried about making mistakes, or getting everything exactly right. They are concerned only with being understood. And they will keep trying until they are. It is the goal that motivates them, and they don't let what people might think get in their way.

This is how successful people learn. They aren't any cleverer than everybody else – it's just that they're comfortable making mistakes if it means they will be better next time. Don't fear mistakes – they're inevitable. Just make sure you keep making new ones.

This is how you learn fast.

6. Love the process, not just the results

Professor Daniel Chambliss conducted a study among elite swimmers to try to determine what differentiated the elite from the rest. He gave the study the fabulous title, 'The Mundanity of Excellence'.

He found that for the elite the journey became as important as the goal.

> *At the higher levels something of an inversion of attitude takes place [between A grade and C grade swimmers]. What others see as boring and repetitive, say, they [A Grade] find peaceful, even meditative, challenging or therapeutic. It is incorrect to believe that top athletes suffer great sacrifices to achieve their goals . . . they don't see what they do as a sacrifice at all. They like it.*

To succeed, we must see our careers in the same way. If we're always looking to the next job, the next rise, the next promotion, we will be forever dissatisfied. As well as being likely to underperform in our current role. I know people for whom the obsession over the next promotion ultimately derailed their carcers. We must always remember that the most important job is the one we have right now.

This does not mean that we will enjoy every task or every day. Rather, it means we are clear where we want to get to and enjoy the overall process of getting there. And if we stop enjoying it or stop progressing – then we have to do something about it.

7. Focus

To enjoy the process, we must be clear on our goal and feel we are progressing, even if imperfectly, towards it. The most successful businesspeople and entrepreneurs don't get there by accident. They are very clear what they want to achieve and are very focused on getting there. This can undeniably make them uncomfortable people to be around sometimes, but in the cluttered and noisy world of work, it's the only way.

We cannot rely on anybody else to direct our careers, and organisations have a habit of getting in their own and our way. It is all too easy to find ourselves working harder and harder without result. This way disillusion, even burnout, lies.

We must be clear where we'd like to get to and ensure we spend our most valuable resources, our time and energy, wisely in getting ourselves there. Time is the only resource we cannot replace.

8. Be great for the careers of others

One of the most important things to recognise about career success, whatever it means to you, is that you cannot do it on your own. Successful entrepreneurs need large teams of dedicated and passionate people around them; CEOs of billion-dollar companies need the most talented and ambitious people to choose them rather than their competitors.

If you wish to achieve your career goals, you will ultimately need to surround yourself with the very best people. And the very best people are the hardest people to find – not least because everybody wants them. Why should they choose you?

The more successful we are, the more options we have and therefore the more individual agency we have over the choices we make. For us to succeed, talented and ambitious people have to conclude that we are good for their careers. And to stop them leaving we need to keep being good for their careers.

All the most successful people I have met are surrounded by talented and ambitious people who are there not because they have been bullied into it, or because they don't have anywhere better to be. They are there because they believe it is in their interests to be there. And honestly – though it might be hard work, more often than not – because it's fun.

Attitude drives aptitude

Attitude drives aptitude. This is not true in reverse. Aptitude does not necessarily determine (a positive) attitude. Indeed, as Gawande discovered, in some instances a perception of established competence constrains willingness to learn, listen, collaborate and grow.

When thinking about your own career, or that of others for whom you are responsible, what matters most when determining long-term success is a blend of attitude and aptitude. The ideal candidate is not the person who knows the most, but somebody who has the requisite experience and skills, and more importantly the attitude to ensure they learn, grow and contribute to the organisation for the long term. And are able to help others do the same.

Skills, even difficult skills, can be taught and learned. In all careers, learning is a prerequisite for success, and the primary determinant of our ability to learn is our attitude.

CHAPTER 2

How to Get Hired

Before you can become indispensable, you have to get hired. And it is a truism that it's always easier to get a job once you already have one. If you don't have one, whether because you've lost the one you had (I've been there) or because you're searching for your first opportunity, it can feel as though you're sitting alone on the edge of a dancefloor – ignored as everybody swirls and sways just beyond your reach. It can be daunting, lonely and confidence-sapping.

Well, put down your Bacardi and Coke – you're on my dance card.

The employer's perspective

I have hired hundreds of people in my career, and indirectly been responsible for many thousands more. It is an imprecise science. My rule of thumb is that if one in every three people you hire exceeds expectations, another meets them and the third falls short, you're doing well.

Others I've shared this theory with felt that the odds were worse still.

Employers know that hiring is a hit-and-miss exercise, and consequently put significant resources into trying to improve their odds. The paradox of the process is that there are always more applicants than roles, but rarely one single applicant who is clearly more suitable than all others. Choosing who to hire is difficult and unreliable. However, therein lies your opportunity. By being deliberate in your approach, you can find ways to edge your nose in front – and a nose is all it takes.

It is this messy context that explains how most recruitment processes are run. The good news for applicants is that similarities between recruitment processes across different industries mean that hiring is a game with predictable stages and rules. And if there are rules, they can be understood, learned and practised.

A game of two halves

There are two distinct stages to most recruitment processes. To succeed, you need to understand the characteristics of each. In simple terms, the objectives of the first is to determine which of the applicants have the most suitable skills and experience – and reject those who do not. And the second is to determine attitude and cultural fit.

The first is applications.

These will nearly always be in written form, and may include completing some (or all) of the following: a template application form, a question and answer (Q&A) exercise, an evaluative test, a cover letter, and a résumé (curriculum vitae, or CV). For some roles, examples of previous work may be required. An employer may also ask for professional or personal references.

There are usually many more applicants than it is possible for an employer to evaluate in person. The consequence of this is that at the first stage, they are not looking for people who they can hire. That comes next. At the first stage, the applications stage, they're looking for people to exclude. They want to shorten the list to a more manageable number who they can then meet in person.

Therefore, as the candidate, your principal objective during this stage is not to get hired. It is to stay in the game.

This is why small details like typos matter so much. If you are ploughing through hundreds of applications (and remember – it is somebody's job to do so) then decisions can be made for trivial reasons. In. Out. The task of shortening the list is often undertaken by a relatively junior employee, not an expert or someone who is actually responsible for hiring. It is rarely done by the prospective manager for the role, except in quite small companies. Don't make it easy for them to kick you off the list.

For many graduate-level roles, the numbers often quoted on websites and in the press can be daunting (although reliable statistics are harder to find). Nevertheless, it is true that there is nearly always a disparity between the number of applicants and the roles available. It is this disparity that inevitably makes the application stage a numbers game. Success is almost certainly going to require you to apply for multiple roles. However, it is important to remember two things. Firstly: there are concrete methods you can use to improve your chances. And secondly: although employers receive a large number of applications, they do not receive a large number of *high-quality* applications.

The second part of the game is the interview.

The good news is that where the application stage has some of the characteristics of a lottery, the interview stage does not. Interviews are reasonably predictable. Most employers are looking for broadly similar characteristics, which you can strengthen through preparation and practice (two words that will recur throughout this book).

At the interview stage, employers are not seeking to reject, but hire. They have a problem and they want you to be the solution. If they offer you the job, it's not just you who has had a good day – somebody gets to tick a task off their cluttered to-do list.

PART 1: APPLICATIONS

As we've established, there are usually more applicants with the necessary skills than it is possible to meet – so some of them must be rejected. This is why small details and persistence matter so much.

The following tips will help you significantly increase your chances of making it through the application stage and getting selected for an interview.

1. Qualifications

For about 70 per cent of jobs, it does not matter what degree (or other qualifications) you have. What matters more is the quality of the qualification: an A is better than a C; a well-known university more valuable than lesser-known one.

However, qualifications are mostly only relevant when applying for your first job – you are unlikely to get asked about them again, unless they're mid-career, professional qualifications that are required for progress. This is because qualifications up to university level are little more than a proxy measure which employers use to make a guess at your suitability for a role, and/or your future career potential. They're an unreliable guide to future career success, which is why you're unlikely to ever be asked about them again – six months of work is a far more useful guide to future success than your first-class degree in art history. Perhaps even if you want to be an art historian.

Employers have little hard evidence to use when deciding whether to offer you an interview – and they know (or suspect) that many people embellish their applications. Though an imperfect guide, qualifications are at the very least a hard metric and consequently valuable. They imply a preparedness to work hard and an ability to learn – both of which are relevant for all jobs.

2. What do employers want?

The majority of employers are looking for very similar characteristics in the people they hire. These are surprisingly consistent through your career:

- Likeability
- Understanding of how to be a great team member
- Leadership potential (or experience)
- Problem-solving skills
- Good work ethic
- Energy
- Passion
- Enthusiasm
- Resilience

These are what they are attempting to understand during the interview process. However, it is also important to do your best to showcase these strengths at the application stage too. For example, evidence of having worked successfully in teams, or of sticking at a difficult task, are useful nudges that might keep you in the game.

3. Work experience and work placements

When applying for your first job, remember that employers don't want to hire successful students – they want to hire successful employees. The increase in the number of university graduates has made it harder for employers and applicants to use degree qualifications as a means of differentiation.

Consequently, prior work experience and participation in work placement schemes are becoming invaluable when hunting for entry-level jobs, and it doesn't matter too much what that work experience is. If you are passionate about a role in a specific industry, having already worked in that sector is a great way of improving your chances. But the most important point is that a candidate with good-quality work experience will have an advantage over those who do not – irrespective of sector.

Work experience, whether volunteering, waiting tables or fetching coffees on a trading floor can help you find the job you love, or (as happened to me) work out what you definitely don't want to do. It will never be wasted time, and will make you a more interesting, rounded and knowledgeable candidate, offering you differentiation in a cluttered field and providing employers with a practical guide to future performance.

And whatever it is you have done, make sure you get a good written reference. If you don't have one, ask for it – they matter.

4. Résumés and cover letters

A cursory Google search throws up page after page of companies offering support (free and paid) for how to write better résumés and cover letters. You should always be open to advice, but neither is a complicated document and there is no need to pay for help. Save your money: here's all you need to know.

A résumé is simply a fact sheet. Nobody gets hired based on their résumé – although if you screw it up you can certainly get rejected. The principles are straightforward:

- Keep it simple
- Don't use pictures, clipart or photographs (unless you are asked to provide one)
- Use no more than two colours
- Use a maximum of two classic fonts and never use handwritten fonts
- Choose a straightforward template (for example from Google or Word)

Sometimes you will be advised to keep your résumé to a single page, although, as you progress through your career, this will become increasingly difficult. Ultimately, length is less important than the quality of the content. But always avoid filler; it will get you cut.

I have provided a template as an example at the end of this section, but this is simply one I adapted from Word – you can do the same.

*

Whereas your résumé is a fact sheet and so can often be reused largely unchanged, a cover letter will need to be tailored to every application. It should read as though you have written it specifically for that job and should communicate your understanding of the opportunity, your passion for the role and evidence for why you are *the* candidate they need to meet. They are not easy to do well, not least because many people find writing about themselves a little uncomfortable.

Because each one must appear to be bespoke (even if in reality you may be able to reuse some of the material), it is not possible to provide as tight a template for a cover letter as it is for a résumé. Nevertheless, at the end of this section, I have provided a framework you can follow to ensure you give yourself the best possible chance of success. And always remember:

- Tailor each section to the specific job and company.
- Be genuine and confident – let your personality come through.
- Keep it concise. Don't waffle. One great example is better than three poor ones.
- Proofread carefully. A polished letter shows attention to detail. If necessary, ask for help.

No matter how well written they are, a cover letter and résumé are not going to get you a job on their own. But if they are messy or full of typos they can lose you a job, irrespective of how great your experience. Avoid filler and waffle, and sweat the small stuff.

5. Give them what they want

The employer has already told you what they want – there are almost always specific qualities and/or tasks listed in the job description/posting.

Take as much information from the description as you can, and play it back to them – literally. Tell them what they want to hear, using the same language that they have used. You can do this on your résumé, in your cover letter and on application forms. We will return to this at the interview stage.

6. Beware AI

Increasingly, employers are using artificial intelligence (AI) to sift through candidates. The reverse is also true – increasingly, candidates are using AI to put together applications. Be warned: it is an unreliable friend. It may help supplement the process, but it's not good enough to do the job on its own. Make sure to include enough of you in your application, and that it doesn't look like a generic AI-generated document, because those will be the first to be cut.

In order to succeed you're likely to have to make multiple applications for different jobs. The temptation is to treat these as cut-and-paste documents, but you must resist this. The way you make yours stand out is to make it as specific and relevant as possible. Therefore, though you should not re-invent the wheel each time, you will need to do your best to make each application feel specific to that employer alone.

7. Whatever the outcome, get feedback

If you're selected for interview, remember to send your prospective employer a short, polite email saying: *Thank you very much, I'm super-excited and can't wait for what's next.*

If you get rejected (and you inevitably will be sometimes), you should politely ask for constructive feedback. Getting rejected is shitty, but it happens to us all. By asking for feedback, you can at least learn a little along the way – and you'll be a bit better prepared next time. Here's a simple template:

> Dear [employer],
>
> I was disappointed to learn that I have not made it through to the interview stage of the recruitment process. I would really appreciate any feedback you can give me that will help me with future opportunities.
>
> Also, I would still love to work with [company name], so please keep my name on file should future opportunities arise – whether for permanent or temporary roles.
>
> Kind regards,
>
> [Your name]

You can also adapt this if you fall at the interview stage. Sometimes you will get a reply, sometimes not – but it takes no time and is worth doing.

It might feel like a long shot, but I can think of several occasions when candidates who were initially rejected, through a little good fortune and persistence, have ended up getting the job. You just never know. Persistence pays off.

Template résumé
Chris Hirst

+44 xxxx xxxxxx | chris@chris-hirst.com
British, based in London
www.chris-hirst.com

Summary

A global CEO with a proven track record of business transformation and M&A integration delivering significant top- and bottom-line growth.

Co-founder of AAR eLearning and keynote speaker.

Author of the award-winning and best-selling books *No Bullsh*t Leadership* and *No Bullsh*t Change* – and sometime host of the No Bullsh*t Leadership podcast.

Education

Harvard Business School – Advanced Management Programme

Brasenose College, Oxford University – MEng (Engineering Science)

Haydon Bridge County High School – Northumberland

Experience

2015–2022 Havas Creative Group, Global CEO & UK Group CEO
Lorem ipsum Quisque blandit dolor vel ullamcorper fringilla. Etiam ut ultricies nibh.

2010–2015 Grey London, CEO
Lorem ipsum Quisque blandit dolor vel ullamcorper fringilla. Etiam ut ultricies nibh.

Writing

*No Bullsh*t Leadership* – business book of the year in 2020.

*No Bullsh*t Change* – shortlisted business book of the year in 2024.

Interests

County standard tennis; keen but haphazard golfer and aging squash player.

Happy-go-lucky guitarist.

(Part-time) author.

History geek, theatre lover, book devourer, non-stats-based cricket enthusiast and obsessive about understanding how things work.

Template cover letter

Introduction:

Objective: Set the stage with your current status and a brief overview of who you are. Tailor this to the job you're applying for.

Example: 'As a marketing professional with over five years of experience driving customer engagement and brand growth . . .'

Example: 'As a recent graduate with a degree in Computer Science, I bring a fresh perspective and a strong foundation in software development.'

Statement of intent:

Objective: A concise summary of what you offer. This should be personal, showcasing a core strength aligned with the role.

Example: 'I am passionate about how data-driven strategies can transform brand awareness and build stronger audience connections.'

Example: 'I thrive in roles that require innovative problem-solving, bringing creative solutions to complex technical challenges.'

Why this company:

Objective: Express why you are specifically drawn to this organisation and how their mission resonates with you. Add a genuine compliment to reinforce your interest.

Example: 'I admire [Company Name]'s commitment to innovation and believe my background in successful new product launches is a great fit with your culture.'

Example: 'Your dedication to sustainability and ethical business practices inspires me, and I am eager to help further these goals.'

Relevant experience:

Objective: Highlight your experience relevant to the role, using specific examples and language from the job posting.

Example: 'In my previous role at XYZ Corp, I managed a cross-functional team to launch a campaign that increased user engagement by 30 per cent, echoing the collaborative leadership emphasised in your job description.'

Example: 'As an intern at ABC Ltd, I streamlined internal processes by implementing an automated scheduling tool, which reduced administrative hours by 15 per cent.'

Unique contributions:

Objective: Showcase what sets you apart – skills, awards, languages, or unique experiences. Keep it relevant to the job at hand.

Example: 'I am fluent in Spanish and certified in Google Analytics. I work hard, love to help teams solve problems and learn quickly.'

Example: 'Having published articles in peer-reviewed journals, I bring experience, expertise and the ability to communicate complex ideas effectively to diverse audiences.'

Education (if relevant):

Objective: Mention educational achievements that directly support your candidacy.

Example: 'With a degree in Environmental Science, I am well prepared to contribute to your sustainability initiatives.'

Example: 'As a recent MBA graduate specialising in finance, I am equipped to drive strategic decision-making in high-paced environments.'

Conclusion:

Objective: Close with gratitude and a forward-looking statement of belief, tying back to your qualifications and enthusiasm for the role.

Example: 'Thank you for considering my application. I believe my strategic mindset and enthusiasm for [Industry/Field] will add value to [Company Name]'s ongoing projects, and I look forward to the opportunity to discuss this further.'

Example: 'I appreciate your time and consideration, and I am confident that my expertise and passion will make a meaningful contribution to your team.'

PART 2: INTERVIEWS

Interviews are not a lottery. Success comes from preparation and practice, not luck. After several decades in CEO roles, I've seen it all – and the candidates who stand out aren't necessarily the smartest or the most experienced. They're the ones who've done the work.

For employers, the first stage of the process is about shortening the list, but interviews are about meeting the people they want to hire. Here's how to make sure that person is you, as well as some common pitfalls that you should avoid unless you want to get dumped on the slush pile before you've even begun.

1. Reasons to be positive

The most important thing to remember when you walk into an interview is that the employer is investing their time and resources into hiring someone because they have a problem – and they really do think (indeed, hope) that you might be the solution. They want to hire you; they want to see you succeed (even if sometimes it doesn't feel that way). The fact that you're being interviewed means that they have already concluded you have the necessary skills and experience. What they now need to do is get to know you.

Interview success is 90 per cent perspiration, 10 per cent inspiration. They're a competitive event, and effective preparation will give you significant advantage, not least because many others do not. The fact that you're reading this right now puts you ahead of many.

Remember, you have every reason to be confident.

2. Understand the process

Almost every interview process involves more than one meeting, sometimes meeting the same person several times, sometimes an assortment of different people. There is no pattern: they may be spread over a long period of time, or all condensed into one day; you may be there alone or you may be there alongside other candidates – as is typical with graduate recruitment processes.

If you have multiple meetings scheduled for the same day, beware: you are being evaluated the whole time – even if you're told you're not. That gossipy person who sits next to you at lunch, they're going to be asked what they think of you – so stay switched on.

In some processes, the first interview may be different to the others. Occasionally, this may also be a stage where people are cut. In these situations, the first interview may be with somebody from the HR department tasked with confirming that you are who you claimed to be in your application. If that's the case, this first interview is primarily a skills check – so be prepared to answer questions about your résumé. If you have been economical with the truth, you'd better have your story straight.

More often than not, you will be shuttled between different people in whatever order their diaries allow. In this case, you will have to treat each meeting as a stand-alone event, and simply aim to perform at your best each time.

3. Do your research

The easiest way to improve your chances is through effective background research. It can give you a significant competitive advantage, not least because most people don't do it well. Being properly prepared is also the best way to ensure you feel confident going into the meeting – and, in interviews, confident people perform better. There are a number of straightforward things you should do:

The job description

The job description doesn't just tell you about the role and its responsibilities – it also tells you about the kind of person the employer is looking for. Make sure to plan ways to play the description back to them in the interview, along with evidence and examples.

LinkedIn

If you haven't got a LinkedIn profile, you should set one up. These days, it is odd not to have one. Make sure it looks professional and is up-to-date. Look up the people you are meeting and learn what you can about them.

Open-source information/website

Look at the company's website, learn about their products, read the executive summary of the annual report, study their competitors and relevant trade publications. All this will add an immense weight to your answers in the interview, providing you with a wealth of information that you can reference.

Glassdoor

The Glassdoor website can give you a flavour of the company, though I would take everything with a pinch of salt. More usefully, it may have a section on their recruitment process. If you're lucky, it might even include the types of questions you may be asked in the interview.

4. Preparation, preparation, preparation

You should pull together all that you've learned and package it in a way that is useful to you in the interview. Success is not going to be a result of simply regurgitating all that you've researched – it will require you to use relevant aspects of that knowledge when answering the questions you are asked.

You can never prepare for every question – and the fact that you may well meet an eclectic array of people makes it even more difficult. Nevertheless, with a little thought, you can ensure you are well placed to give an intelligent response irrespective of what you are asked.

Do not just assume it'll be alright on the night – especially if you have not attended many interviews before.

5. Stone-cold classic interview questions

Though you cannot prepare for every question, you can and should prepare for the questions you think you're most likely to be asked. This is very important. Having knowledge is not the same as structuring answers under pressure. So take this part seriously! You can customise your own list, but here are my suggested ten stone-cold classics:

1. Tell me about yourself.
2. What are your greatest strengths?
3. What are your greatest weaknesses?
4. Why do you want to come and work here?
5. Tell me about a time that you faced a challenge at work. How did you handle it?

6. Where do you see yourself in five years' time?
7. Describe a time you worked brilliantly in a team.
8. Why are you leaving your current job?
9. How do you prioritise your work?
10. Do you have any questions for us?

Carefully prepare and practise your answers. Write them down; say them out loud. If you just skim the above list and think, *I got it*, the chances are you haven't.

The more you practise, the better your answers will get and the more likely you are to remember them under pressure. And remember, your objective when answering is not to be 'right', it is to tell them what they want to hear and/or land the key points you want them to understand about you. Doing this well takes careful thought, preparation and practice.

6. Practise

Practising interviews can be difficult, but there's an easy way to do it. And the effort is definitely worthwhile. Once you have your sample questions and answers written down, simply ask a friend or colleague to test you on them – as you would when revising for an exam. You don't have to try to exactly replicate an interview scenario; this is very difficult to do. However, practice is a great way of developing your muscle memory, and of getting friendly feedback to improve your answers.

Saying something out loud to somebody else is always different to just thinking it through on your own. If you want to significantly increase your chances of success, do not skip this step.

7. Have you got any questions for us?

Every interviewer asks this question. It is much-mythologised, but my advice is that you shouldn't overthink it or give it too much weight. However, it is important you have something prepared – people expect it. If you have genuine questions, ask them. That said, my advice is not to ask either of these two questions during an interview:

- *What is the salary?*
  This is a reasonable question, but if you haven't already been told, now is not the time. Some employers have a weird hang-up about it – so don't ask. Yet.
- *Do you offer flexible working (or variations)?*
  Like it or not, flexible working remains a touchy subject for some employers. Like the question of salary, it is definitely a reasonable one – but my advice is not to ask it in an interview unless you feel very sure of the company's position on the matter.

Both questions can wait until you're offered the job. At that point, you can ask and if necessary negotiate from a position of relative strength. Remember: if they've offered you the job, you are the solution to a problem for them. They've spent a lot of time and effort getting to this point – so they want it to work. You are not without agency.

If you don't like the answers at that stage, you can always say no to the job, but it is always better to ask about salary and flexibility from a position of strength.

Aside from those, here are ten example questions you can use if you need a little inspiration. Always have two or three up your sleeve.

1. *Can you tell me more about the team I'd be working with?* Demonstrates your interest in collaboration and understanding the team dynamics.
2. *What does success look like for this role in the first 30, 60 or 90 days?* Shows you're proactive and career-focused.
3. *How would you describe the company culture here?* A great way to gauge if the company's values and environment align with your preferences. And whether they can articulate them.
4. *What do you personally enjoy most about working here?* Always an interesting question to ask, you never know what answer you'll get.
5. *Are there any challenges the team or company is currently facing that this role can help address?* Demonstrates that you're business-minded and solution-oriented.
6. *Can you share some examples of career development opportunities within the company?* Shows you're interested in growing and contributing long-term.
7. *What are the next steps in the interview process?* A practical and useful question, it shows forward-thinking and confidence.
8. *How do you see this role evolving in the next couple of years?* Shows you're thinking about the future and potential for growth.

9. *What's the biggest challenge facing the company right now, and how does this role contribute to addressing it?* Shows a strategic mindset and a genuine interest in the company's success.

10. *Is there anything about my background or interview today that gives you pause or leaves you with questions?* A bold and confident option. Just be ready to react.

8. No-nos

You probably think you don't need to read a section that lists easy-to-avoid mistakes, but I've included it because I have seen candidates stumble on every single one.

They're easy to avoid – so make sure you do.

- Don't be late. It is better to be an hour early than one minute late. The ideal is to be about fifteen minutes early.
- You should dress appropriately for the role. If you're not sure, dress slightly smarter than you would on a normal working day.
- Do not bad-mouth your current employer, the other candidates or people you have been previously interviewed by.
- Don't chew gum.
- Don't lie. It is better to say you don't know than to lie. If you get found out, you'll be out.
- Clean hands, clean clothes, clean hair!

Creating an uneven playing field

Getting hired is more art than science, but it's not something over which you have no control. It is a game and the rules can be learned. Preparation and practice will significantly improve your chances.

Sometimes the raw statistics (numbers of candidates, for example) can be daunting, but what you must remember is that not all candidates are equal – and not all applications are of a high quality. To win you must seek out competitive advantage. The principles outlined in this chapter do not guarantee success every time, but if you follow them and learn as you go, you'll get there. I guarantee.

And once you have a job, it is far easier to get the next one.

CHAPTER 3

Understanding Teams

To succeed in our careers, we need to understand how to lead teams and what it means to be a great team member.

The smallest indivisible unit of an organisation is not the individual, it is the team. All organisations are made up of multiple interlocking teams and we are nearly all members of teams throughout our careers, and as such rarely act in isolation.

As we progress through our careers, when we change jobs, when the inevitable head office shake-up finally reaches us, we move from team to team, switch from leader to leader. It is such a universal experience that we take it for granted. Yet despite the ubiquity of teams and the language that surrounds them, most organisations spend almost no time thinking about what is required for a team to perform brilliantly, what it means to be a great team member and what distinguishes the most effective team leaders.

There are three universal measures we can use to understand our experiences as a member of the many teams to which we will belong throughout our careers:

1. How good is the team at performing its core tasks?

2. Does the team provide a positive or negative working environment for its members?

3. Is the team professionally rewarding, and does it further its members' ambitions?

It can often be the case that two teams working on the same tasks within the same organisation, when judged against these criteria, are polar opposites. And it's not an abstract difference – the members of each can experience unequal pay rises, job satisfaction and rates of career progression. Team performance accelerates or retards individual careers as well as business performance. That this is so obvious makes it all the more surprising that the majority of organisations pay so little heed to how great teams are formed, sustained and led.

It is possible for unhappy teams to perform well and it is certainly possible for happy teams to underperform. Being in a bad team doesn't ruin your career and being in a great team sometimes means the wrong people get promoted. However, in general, there is a clear correlation between the contentedness of a team's members, the team's performance and individual progress. It is common sense that strong teams find a virtuous circle of positive results, leading to a greater sense of personal achievement, increased confidence and therefore a further improvement in performance.

Ultimately the most significant determinant of whether a team will be great or poor is its leadership. Poor leaders will list all the reasons that fate has conspired against them, effective leaders always find a way.

You will find yourself a member of many teams through your career. In time, if you don't already, you will lead them. The principles of what makes great teams work are universal, and good habits practised and ingrained early will put you in good stead throughout your career.

What makes a great team?

'Team' is one of those words we throw around loosely to describe any kind of assembly of people, but in fact a team can be very specifically defined:

> *A group of people with a recognised leader, whose members have a mix of both complementary and appropriate skills, and who collaborate effectively in order to achieve their collective objective.*

So much, so obvious. However, the reality often falls a long way short of this.

For the majority of us, our first experience of work was to be assigned to a team. It is likely, however, that the person in charge had little or no formal training to help them understand what leadership is or how to do it well. Furthermore, your new colleagues were not a hand-picked, carefully chosen and complementary group (as all business books say teams should be), but rather, a group of people thrown together by the vagaries of recruitment, promotion, rotation and time.

In the real world, most teams are in a state of permanent evolution. Take sports teams, for example. A Premier League football team clearly and easily fits my definition, but it is also a mongrel. It inevitably consists of players who are at different stages of their career, who have different relationships with the manager and who, unless the manager has been in post for a long time, were brought into the team under previous regimes.

The consequence of this is that the idealised definition of 'team' as a carefully hand-picked group of perfectly balanced, complementary and motivated individuals brought together for a specific task, almost never exists. More commonly teams are an eclectic assembly of individuals with quite differing experiences, motivations and ambitions. Good leaders are those who find a way to make mongrel teams excel.

There are six characteristics that all great teams possess.

1. Clarity of objective

It is impossible to get there if you don't know where you're going.

Great teams have a very clear understanding of what it is they are trying to achieve. A common problem in business is that this is often assumed rather than made explicit, with the consequence that different team members pull in different directions, often prioritising their own individual responsibilities or ambitions ahead of the collective goal.

Great teams are aligned behind a clearly and universally understood objective, with all members committed to how exactly it will be achieved.

2. Clarity of individual objectives

All teams are made up of individuals. The skill of the leader is to make the whole greater than the sum of the parts. A successful team comprises great individuals who see the fulfilment of the team's objectives as wholly aligned with the fulfilment of their own ambitions.

Members must, at different times, be both selfish and unselfish. They must be clear what it is they personally wish to achieve and at the appropriate points fight their corner to ensure they get what they need. But at other times they must put the needs of others and the collective first.

Crucially, everybody in the team must be sure of their role in achieving the team's objective. If they are not (and this is not unusual), they cannot contribute to best effect. Many consequently feel a sense of dislocation or even isolation. A good way of understanding what your role is, is to ask this question of your team leader:

What are the most important tasks I should focus on in order for us to succeed?

The answer to this question will be your specific personal targets, set within the context of the wider team goal.

In a good team, everybody is clear about their and everybody else's role; they're clear what their personal objectives are and understand how the achievement of the collective goal will benefit them.

3. Great communication

Communication is the most underappreciated asset of a successful team (and indeed a successful career). Great teams encourage honest, respectful and frequent communication between their members.

In a strong team, communication is not simply a top-down activity. Team members must communicate effectively with each other, both formally (e.g., in presentations and emails) and informally (e.g., over a coffee). The benefits of great communication are almost limitless: it's how we build and sustain relationships, how we understand each other, how we deal with conflict, how we learn and how we stay on track.

Respectful disagreement is the torture test for an effective team. If things aren't being said, it doesn't mean they aren't being thought (or moaned about, off-stage). The inability to openly disagree magnifies the corrosive effects of office politics as well as being a major barrier to problem-solving and decision-making – among much else.

A measure of an effective team is whether its members can disagree without falling out. In the best teams, everybody has a voice and everybody is listened to, even if they disagree. Perhaps especially if they disagree. Unfashionable, I know.

4. A culture that elevates

Culture is what differentiates great teams from the rest. It is the environment the leader creates in order for their team to outperform. It is the defining experience for all of us in any organisation. In effective teams, the desired culture is made explicit and universally understood.

A leader's behaviour determines their team's culture – whether that's conscious and deliberate or not. What they do matters far more than what they say in shaping the behaviours of those for whom they are responsible. For this reason, different teams in the same organisation will have different cultures, perhaps linked by an organisational red thread, but distinct nevertheless. Though the organisation-wide culture will influence that of an individual team, it will not define it. Leaders must take conscious responsibility for the culture in their teams.

Culture is defined by behaviours. Everybody in the team must be clear on their collectively agreed-upon behaviours. This is not difficult to do, but is very often overlooked, ignored or assumed – meaning that, in reality, everybody simply does things their way. Even if the organisation is clear about what its culture and the associated behaviours are, every individual team should take the time to discuss and understand what that means for them in practice.

In effective teams, everybody should be clear on how members are expected to behave and hold each other to that standard. This will determine how conflicts are resolved, how feedback is given, how to celebrate successes, how to handle failures and how to respect each other's boundaries. These 'Teamship' rules (a term coined by World Cup-winning coach Sir Clive Woodward) are easy to implement and extremely effective. Yet the vast majority of teams do not take such an enlightened approach.

It is a team's shared behaviours that ultimately drive its performance.

5. Collective responsibility

A great team looks out for each other. Poor teams don't. This can be seen in many aspects of its day-to-day business, but is perhaps thrown into sharpest relief at the extremes: managing failure and celebrating success.

Both are collective experiences, yet in poor teams they very often become focused on individuals, either due to a search for a scapegoat or in the pursuit of individual glory. Both rapidly undermine a team's coherence.

By definition, a team's success or failure isn't a consequence of individual actions, but of the performance of the whole. It is inevitable that things will go wrong from time to time. Indeed, we have already argued that failure and mistakes are desirable; progress is impossible without them. Teams need to not simply be forgiving, but accept that these are the price to be paid in order to achieve their goals. The fear of failure is not just an individual constraint, but a collective problem that ambitious teams must overcome lest it hold them back. It is a poor team's inability to manage setbacks in a supportive way, and to learn from them, that ultimately stops it achieving its goals.

Teams that out-perform may make more mistakes than those who stumble anonymously along, but where they differ is how they support individuals through these and learn from them to ensure they all do better next time. This is how all progress happens.

6. Trust and inclusion

Great teams maintain high-trust environments that ensure all their members have clear roles and are able to speak up and be heard.

They are also diverse environments, containing people of different backgrounds, cultures, ages, ambitions, skills and experiences.

On the face of it, ensuring everybody can contribute sounds simple enough, yet we know from experience it often doesn't happen. Some people are naturally outspoken, some introverted, some over-confident, some under-confident. No one personality type is more 'right' than another, no one type of voice more useful in achieving the team's goals. But without deliberate and continuous effort, important, wise, even expert voices can be drowned out, or remain unheard, to the detriment of the team and the individuals concerned.

Though a common problem, a lack of trust and inclusion isn't difficult to overcome. But it does require a conscious effort from the leader to ensure it becomes an accepted part of the culture. I have worked with many serious-minded and conscientious leaders for whom this is a particular blind spot.

Building a sense of community must be a continuous and conscious activity – and a primary responsibility of the senior members of the team. If somebody doesn't speak up, it's not necessarily because they don't have something to say. Not having the space to say it is not their problem to solve – it's the leader's.

Failing to do this is one of the most common reasons teams don't reach their full potential.

What makes a great team member?

Learning how to become an indispensable team member is the beating heart of this book.

If you aren't already, very soon you will find yourself responsible for others. You will be the leader whose influence will be so formative for those who report to you. However, throughout our careers, irrespective of how senior we become, we will also always be team members. The majority of people are team leaders, team members, bosses, colleagues, employers and employees all at the same time. Even as a CEO of a billion-dollar business, I was a team member and had a boss. Situations change but the principles don't.

What makes a great team member is not a function of experience or age. It is possible to become indispensable to your colleagues even as the most junior person in the room. However, the challenge is that often we are taught the functional aspect of a new role, but not how to become an integral part of the team we have just joined. We gain aptitude but are left to guess at attitude. Yet when colleagues talk about each other, it is most commonly people's attitude that is praised or criticised, not their aptitude. We all do it. We'll say, 'I just love Anna's energy' or 'John's such a dick'. These aren't related to whether Anna's a better salesperson than John, but rather our experience of them as fellow team members.

We want to work with people who we want to be around. People who make our lives easier, better, happier and more enjoyable. People who bring the energy rather than drain it. People who, in the storm preceding a high-pressure meeting, step up and say, 'Let me take care of that.'

And that's what they want from us too. Here's how to do it.

1. Look out for others

The first and most important responsibility of team members is to look out for each other; to have each other's backs. If all teams only did this one thing, it would be transformational. Great teams do not simply materialise but are a deliberate and carefully maintained construct. It is no coincidence that this behaviour is number one on my list.

All of us need help, support, advice and a kind word from time to time. The best people I have worked with appear at your side just as the weight becomes unbearable, to offer their help or to simply ask if you're doing okay. Everybody can do this. And all teams should be explicit that this is expected of their members.

Camaraderie is the connective tissue that holds a great team together.

2. Be world class at the things that require no talent

One of the best pieces of career advice I ever heard was this. Very little in this book requires any great talent to master; with diligence and will, anybody can do all of it. It requires no talent to turn up on time, to listen respectfully to others, to compose a clear meeting agenda, to rehearse to ensure you make your points clearly and concisely, to do the necessary background work to support your opinions, to chair a meeting well or to ask a colleague if they are okay.

Yet – these are the things that connect us, build trust and mutual respect. Characteristics that all great teams need.

3. Do what you say you'll do

This requires no elaboration. If you want to become a trusted team member, you need to be somebody who does what they say they'll do. If there is a reason you can't – own it. If you need help, ask.

Most of your working life, even for CEOs, will not be made up of great transformational moments, but rather of lots of small everyday acts, from emails and corridor conversations to presentations and status meetings. Once you've done a few, even board meetings become routine. These things are the meat and potatoes of the working day. The way we build trust is to consistently deliver against the commitments we make, small as well as big.

If you say you're going to do it – do it.

The people who do are those we learn to trust. For our careers, the return on being that person is significant. When the big moments arise – the key projects, the new opportunities, the promotions – it is to trusted people we turn.

Whenever I find myself in a new role, the first thing I do is put people in place around me who I know will do what they say – who, above all else, I trust. It is the principal piece of advice I give to anybody new to a senior role. And it's not just me. When new managers are appointed to Premier League football clubs, they never come alone. They always bring a team with them – people they know they can trust from day one.

Too many people over-promise, under-deliver and then avoid the consequences. I would not want them on my team and you wouldn't want them on yours.

People who do what they say are the first names on the team sheet.

4. Be respectful

Respect is earned through how we treat others:

- Listen when others speak
- Invite people in if they're on the outside
- Scrutinise other people's ideas, not their personalities
- Assume goodwill
- Turn up on time
- Remember that other people's lives and experiences are different to your own
- Expect (maybe even encourage) a difference of opinions
- Find the positives in another's opinion or work before you find the negatives

- Don't be the devil's advocate unless you're specifically asked to be

I knew a colleague who had a screensaver that read: *Remember: you might be wrong*.

The best way to earn respect is to behave how we would wish to be treated.

5. Be a radiator not a drain

The people we most want in our team are those who bring energy to the room. The people we least want are those who suck the energy from the room.

It is always the same person I think of when I give this advice. When Katie first joined us, she was one of the most junior people on the team, though she progressed very rapidly – and for good reason. What made her remarkable was that she had an ability to spot the things that nobody else was doing and to quietly and efficiently get them done – or chivvy others to do the same. She seemed to be unfazed by her position in the hierarchy and simply hunted out the places where she could add value, bringing a positive energy and can-do attitude to every situation. Even if that just meant getting everybody a cup of tea at 1.00 a.m. the morning before the pitch – just as things were getting fractious. She had an ego, but was apparently ego-less – and everybody loved her.

The room warmed up and a solution seemed closer when she was present. It cooled and slowed when she left.

Nobody has a good day every day. Nobody feels full of energy all the time. Work is only part of our lives and it is impossible to neatly segment our emotions. But it is possible to be a person whose default setting is to be proactive, supportive and solution-focused. This is the energy teams need, and being that person will make you the person everybody wants on their team. The tougher things get, the more valuable you become. Energy doesn't simply warm rooms; it helps teams find their way through.

6. Be accountable

Somewhat counter-intuitively, owning up to mistakes is a powerful way to build trust, because everybody knows that things go wrong sometimes. Nobody welcomes it, but it's inevitable. As we've established, failure is not just an occupational hazard, but a prerequisite for success. As such, it is a necessity for ambitious people and teams. Which is not to say it isn't painful when it happens. Putting your hand up when things go wrong can take courage, but the best people in the best-run teams take responsibility and are respected and valued by their colleagues as a result. They are honest when things go wrong, quick to learn from their mistakes, and unafraid to get stuck in to find a solution.

7. Seek feedback

I worked with a very successful leader once who continually demanded feedback. 'Don't give me the platitudes,' she'd say, 'I want to hear the bad stuff, I want to know where I need to improve.' I was always kind of in awe because most of us find listening to the things we need to do better uncomfortable. Even when it's done well.

Most organisations have an annual formal review process. These can be useful, but they are often cumbersome and take up so much time that they end up being little more than rushed box-ticking exercises. What should be for the benefit of the employee becomes a task to be got through with minimum pain for both parties. Therefore, if you're interested in your own career, do not rely solely on these.

A more useful way is to seek informal feedback from those you work with. Be respectful of their time; don't make them fill in forms. Instead, help them understand that you want feedback because you want to be better at helping them achieve their goals, and because you want to learn in order to achieve your own.

The best way is to keep it informal, perhaps over a coffee with your manager every six months. You might be pleasantly surprised how easy and useful this can be. Ask simple questions such as:

- What should I stop, start and continue doing?
- How can I be more useful to the team?
- What am I best at?
- In what ways do I add most value?
- What should my areas of personal focus be for the next six months?
- What do you need most from me?

At every session, ask just a couple of questions, write down the answers, email them to your manager and review them next time. Make it easy and useful for both of you.

Don't overthink it. You'll be surprised what comes out and about the positive impact this initiative will have on your role within the team and how you are perceived. And of course, your own rate of development.

If you take your career development seriously, so will everybody else.

Sweep the sheds

Most projects and businesses are not propelled forward by flashes of blinding inspiration from crazy mavericks or reclusive geniuses, but by groups of people working together, in supportive teams, towards collectively understood objectives; teams where everybody knows their role and is valued for it. If this sounds mundane, it is anything but. Being part of a high-performing team is an exhilarating experience that can supercharge your career.

In order to thrive, teams need mutually supportive members, people who embrace the culture, who work hard and who lighten the room when they walk in. They also need people who know what their jobs within the team are, and who take pride in performing them well.

In his book *Legacy*, which details the strategies behind the most successful sports team of all time – New Zealand's rugby union All Blacks – author James Kerr relates what has become a famous anecdote. After a resounding win, he describes the scene as a team packed with World Cup winners is about to leave the dressing room:

> *Something happens that you might not expect. Two of the senior players – one an international player of the year, twice – each pick up a long-handled broom and begin to sweep.*

The team calls it 'sweeping the sheds'. Kerr continues:

> *Sweeping the sheds. Doing it properly. So no-one else has to. Because no-one looks after the All Blacks. The All Blacks look after themselves.*

It's a powerful and moving story. In great teams, members do whatever needs to be done. No job is too small or unimportant. They are proud and self-sufficient. They have each other's backs.

Great team members put the needs of the team and their colleagues first. People who understand this become indispensable team members from their first day. That few seem to understand this is perhaps your greatest opportunity.

CHAPTER 4

Leadership: Difficult, But Not Complicated

Leadership is how things get done, how problems are solved and how we help those around us. Great leaders accelerate our careers and poor leaders hold us back.

Every time we are promoted it means greater responsibility and that invariably means being responsible for ever-increasing numbers of people. Therefore, leadership is not simply one skill among many that we must learn in order to succeed, its mastery is the single most important factor in determining our career success. It helps us control the future direction of our careers, is central to how quickly we achieve our goals and it makes us better able to help those we work for and with achieve theirs. Its three core pillars – clarity, action and culture – will form a *leitmotif* for this book.

The greatest and most damaging fallacy that surrounds the subject of leadership is that there is a specific 'leadership type'. Though a widely held belief, it is fundamentally wrong. The idea that you either 'have it or you don't' serves only to inhibit and exclude so many from fulfilling their career potential. There is no leadership type; it is a skill that can be learned and mastered by everybody, and it's never too early (or too late) to learn. Wherever you are in your career, understanding leadership matters to you right now.

However, though everybody can, in theory, learn to be an effective leader, very few do. In the majority of organisations, leadership development is done badly and the way most of us learn to lead is on the job – from seeing it done well or poorly by others. This makes it something of a lottery.

Who is a leader?

The majority of leaders are not presidents, chairwomen or CEOs. Instead, this is my definition:

A leader is anybody who has people they are responsible for.

This means that many people find themselves in leadership roles from very early in their careers. My own experience was typical; I found myself running a small team after about eighteen months of work. However, neither I nor the organisation I worked for saw me as a leader, and I was offered little support in learning how to do it well. Nevertheless, I was the most important person in the (working) lives of the people I was responsible for.

Once we run a team, the key determinant of our rate of career progress ceases to be what we can achieve on our own, and instead becomes the results achieved by our team. This is why leadership matters to us all.

Leadership is a doing word

Leadership is the navigation of a group of people from a defined state in the present to a different and clearly defined state that exists in the future.

Leadership is not fine speeches, clever presentations or big ideas. Leaders may need to do all of those things sometimes, but they are not leadership. Effective leaders fix stuff, get stuff done, fail, fly and lift others. They're flawed and human – perhaps sometimes uncomfortable, demanding and impatient; they might not know the right words or fit in. But they have the courage to give it a go.

I have written extensively about leadership and little else will give you such a high career return-on-investment as developing your understanding of the subject. What follows are the three most important aspects of modern leadership. They will serve as the foundation stones of your future success.

1. Clarity

The Leadership Equation

A leader's impact is made up of two components, linked by the Leadership Equation. If you remember nothing more about leadership than this, you won't go far wrong.

Leadership Impact = Clarity x Action

You cannot reach your destination if you don't know where you're trying to get to. This applies personally and professionally. As leaders, we must be clear on the challenges, opportunities, risks and rewards of our current situation. And we must be clear where we intend to take our team (or ourselves).

Understanding is the prelude to solving

No team or organisation can stand still. It is a myth that team performance can be measured in the three states of growth, status quo and decline. In practice, only two exist: growth and decline. If you're not moving forward, you're going backwards. This is why successful leadership is a constant process of change – not necessarily transformation, but change. It is the continual search for improvement, growth or victory.

To succeed, leaders must have clarity over what it is they are striving to achieve. They must be able to explain to their stakeholders (e.g. team members, bosses, customers, clients or shareholders) the why, where and how:

- **Why** action is needed
- **Where** they wish to lead their team to
- **How** they intend to get there

Clarity is the requirement to understand their current situation, being able to describe a compelling future, and the path they intend to follow between the two. Crucially, leaders must ensure that all those around them are clear also. They have to help their stakeholders understand that change isn't just desirable, but that it is in their personal interests. Effective leaders need to be good communicators.

Strategy is a means of describing a leader's intended journey towards their destination. It is a word fetishised in business, but though important is usually not difficult to do. Indeed, you should be wary of complicated strategies; the more complicated they are, the more likely they are to fail. Not least because people may not understand them or their role in making them a reality.

Many leaders misunderstand the role of strategy. They think the production of strategies is a sign of their leadership virility. It isn't. A strategy is a map, ideas on paper or computer screens – and an important tool to help a leader achieve their goal. Nevertheless, it is not leading. Many businesses don't lack for strategies; in fact, they have too many. What they lack is people prepared to get up from their chair and begin to make them happen. This is leadership.

Leading ourselves

We usually only think about leadership as something we do to others, but many of the principles of leadership can be applied equally to ourselves. Clarity is critical for leading others, but it's also important as we manage our own careers.

It's normal to not know what it is you'd like to be doing in ten or even five years' time. If you do – more power to you. Go for it. But you should not worry if you do not. You should, however, have clarity over your short- and medium-term ambitions if you wish to progress. If you don't know what it is you're trying to get from your current job, you can hardly complain if others (your boss, for example) don't either. Nor can you be surprised if those with greater clarity get promoted ahead of you.

Your ambitions needn't be complicated. They might be as straightforward as getting a promotion within a given timeframe, earning a certain amount of money, gaining a qualification or accreditation, joining a different department or getting a job in a particular industry or company.

If you hate your job, you need a clear plan for what you are going to do about it. If you love your job, you need a clear plan for how you are going to make the most of all it offers you. Whatever your ambitions, all plans are fallible. There will be setbacks, you'll change your mind, new opportunities and problems will arise; but without clarity, you'll be directionless.

You should be explicit about your medium-term ambitions with your boss – don't assume they know. Being ambitious is a good thing as long as you are not unreasonable. Even if your boss thinks you're being unrealistic, clarity will enable you to have a more effective conversation. Their disagreeing with you does not mean the death of your dreams; it means you can form a plan, with them or without them, for how they can be achieved.

We are used to the idea of our employers giving us feedback on our progress. Clarity over our personal goals allows us to ask for what we want from them as well as listen to what our boss wants from us. This is perfectly acceptable. Indeed, it's desirable. In a well-run team your ambitions should align with the ambitions of the team. That way, if the collective succeeds, you also succeed.

Having clarity over our goals allows us to focus on the things we need to do in order to achieve them. It is important to remember that the world of work is a competitive environment. If we want a promotion, a pay rise or a new opportunity, we often have to compete with our colleagues for it. This doesn't mean we should behave badly, quite the opposite, but there's no point in pretending that competition doesn't exist. Therefore, clarity matters. The clearer you are, the better able you are to focus, learn from the successes of others (and your own inevitable failures) in order to ultimately get you to where you want to be. It won't be a straight line, the real world never is, but with clarity, you'll get there.

2. Action

Let's go back to the Leadership Equation.

Leadership Impact = Clarity x Action

Clarity is only half of the story.

The point of the equation is that effective leadership requires action. If you want to achieve anything in your career (or in life), you must act, and the most common reason for leadership failure is the failure to do so. This is because getting stuff done is difficult and uncertain. It is comfortable and reassuring to sit in continuous strategy loops, endlessly refining plans and preparing presentations, but the real point of the equation is to remind us that nothing to the left of the X counts without action. An idea cannot be considered great until it has been executed excellently. Without action everything is just words.

Leadership Impact = Clarity x Action
So if Action = 0
Leadership Impact = Clarity x 0
Leadership Impact = 0

For even the most successful leaders, teams and careers, progress is a zigzag at best. Action brings with it the possibility of error and failure, the knowledge of which can inhibit our decision-making. However, the equation also offers liberation. Even if our plans and strategies are imperfect – and they will be – if we bias towards action, we will still create movement. And as leaders, that's our primary objective. Not least because we should remember the alternative. If Action = 0, we are guaranteed to fail.

A decision is a choice we take when we're uncertain of the outcome

We take action by making decisions. There are few things more frustrating and demoralising than working for somebody who is indecisive. People put off making decisions because they fear getting things wrong, yet the deferral of a decision comes with its own costs: no action means no progress, which means failure.

Therefore, leaders must reframe their understanding of decision-making. It is not an opportunity to be right or wrong – the reality will nearly always be somewhere in between. It is instead an opportunity to take control of events and to progress.

A decision is a choice we are faced with where the outcome is uncertain. If we are certain of the outcome, then no decision is required. Poor leaders put off making decisions in the hope that, by delaying, they will achieve certainty. However, by definition, the outcome is unpredictable, which means that prevarication offers rapidly diminishing returns – the only certainty being that too much delay results in failure.

Leaders must be able to achieve effective results in changing environments, against unpredictable forces with imperfect information. It isn't easy. Only by taking decisions can they hope to stay in control of their direction – which is the liberation of the Leadership Equation. Even then, sometimes they may be blown off course. But it's the only way.

The most useful tool I have found to help leaders make real-world decisions is Colin Powell's 40/70 Rule:

> *Don't take action if you have only enough information to give you a less than 40 per cent chance of being right. But if you've waited until you're 70 per cent certain, you've waited too long.*

Don't act in haste, Powell advises, but it is preferable to act quickly and risk error than to wait too long and be proved wrong by default. He encourages leaders to accept the inevitability of occasional error, but to get on with it anyway.

Don't overestimate the value of ideas

Often team members, particularly juniors, become frustrated because they believe their ideas are not being listened to. If this is the case, it's frustrating; all voices should be heard and listened to. However, the value of ideas is misunderstood. We shouldn't ignore them, but nor should we overestimate their worth.

It is easy to have ideas. We all have them all the time. When I worked in advertising, where ideas were our daily currency, I came to realise that no idea can be considered great until it has been executed excellently. It is the transition from brain to page to action that counts – far more than momentary inspiration. Being the person who is able to translate ideas into action is what moves careers and organisations forward.

Obvious though this is, it is very often misunderstood. One of the most universal frustrations in the workplace is the time wasted in meetings where there is a surfeit of talking and an absence of action. In other words, plenty of ideas, but nothing getting done. Organisations may sometimes not want your ideas, but the truth is that's because they often don't need any more ideas from anybody – they already have too many of them. What they lack is people prepared to make some of those ideas happen.

Be that person

Be the person who encourages the team to action. You can do this without being pushy or presumptuous. It will get you noticed and make you invaluable. Ask for:

- Conclusions
- Recommendations
- Timelines
- Budgets
- Milestones
- Allocation of tasks

This is how brilliant ideas become reality, and if you're the person who is always there putting their hand up with an interesting observation *and* taking responsibility for helping work out how to actually get it done – you will rapidly become indispensable.

3. Culture

We should all understand what culture is and why it matters so much at work. It is the defining experience we all have in any organisation to which we belong, whether a large corporation, a school, a start-up or a sports team. An effective culture has a huge impact not just on how we feel, but on how teams perform. It is this that makes great leadership a form of alchemy. Effective leaders are able to inspire a group of people to achieve results that would not otherwise have seemed possible. Yet in many teams and organisations there is no clear understanding of what the culture is or what they would like it to be.

A good way to get an accurate take on what the actual culture is in your team is to ask yourself or a colleague this question:

What do you have to do to get on around here?

An honest answer is a useful and practical description of what matters most to the team and therefore what the real (as opposed to claimed) culture is. What does the answer to this question tell you about the culture of your team?

What is organisational culture?

> *Culture is the environment a leader creates in order for their team to out-perform.*

Culture is best understood not as values, but as behaviours. Culture is how we treat each other, how we respond to successes and failures; conflicts and problems. A team's culture defines how it judges the balance between listening and speaking, supporting and competing, learning and blaming; me and us. Culture may not have a line of its own on the P&L, but it's there in everything a company does.

Poor leaders often dismiss culture as the preserve of the HR department, a soft, squishy intangible that is of little business importance, yet nothing could be further from the truth. The crisis that has befallen the once mighty Boeing after the deaths of 346 people in two Boeing 737 Max crashes sheds the most baleful possible light on the effect of a disastrous change in culture – and the behaviour of management as its primary driver.

In his paper, 'Boeing – Culture Shift, Safety Issues, and Financial Struggles', Dr Vijesh Jain states:

> *Boeing, once revered as an aviation pioneer synonymous with safety and engineering excellence, has faced a tumultuous period marked by safety scandals, plummeting reputation, and staggering financial losses . . .*
>
> *. . . Under CEO Jim McNerney's tenure, Boeing's focus shifted towards maximizing profitability, often at the expense of safety and engineering standards. The relocation of the company's headquarters to Chicago in 2001 symbolized a departure from its Pacific Northwest heritage, distancing top executives from the manufacturing processes and assembly lines . . .*
>
> *. . . Boeing's descent into crisis reached a crescendo with the 737 Max debacle, where flawed design features and manufacturing defects culminated in two catastrophic crashes. Despite mounting evidence of safety concerns after the first crash, Boeing resisted calls for grounding the aircraft, prioritizing production targets over passenger safety. The subsequent grounding of the 737 Max fleet and protracted investigations inflicted substantial financial losses, with Boeing reporting cumulative net losses exceeding $26 billion over five years . . .*

> *. . . Boeing's credibility and market position have been severely undermined, with Airbus emerging as a dominant competitor in commercial aviation.*

The best way to understand culture is as the behaviour of the leader(s). It is primarily determined by what leaders do, not what they say. Despite this, in many organisations, the gap between these two is very great indeed. The actions Boeing's leaders made – relocating the company from its traditional home state – were clear and unmistakable in their cultural intent, and ultimately disastrous in their effect.

I am often told by leaders that though culture is very important, it is all but impossible to change. Nothing could be further from the truth. It can be done very quickly; simply change the behaviour of the leaders (or the leaders themselves) and the culture changes. The real barrier to building a great culture, as opposed to simply enduring the current culture, is people's willingness to take responsibility for their behaviours. Rather than simply throwing their hands in the air and asking what can they possibly do, leaders must take responsibility for their behaviours as the primary driver of the culture in their team.

Even leaders who wish to take culture seriously often believe it is somehow bigger than them, and therefore beyond their control. Yet, by definition, every leader has at least one team they are responsible for and, in their teams, they are the primary determinant of the culture. If you run a team, its culture isn't bigger than you – it *is* you.

Therefore, organisations, unless they are very small, do not have a homogenous culture. All teams have a distinct culture, because all teams have different leaders. That is why culture in a large organisation is better understood as an aggregate of many micro-cultures. Of course there will be commonalities, but there will also be significant differences. It is common for teams in the same organisation to have very different characteristics and consequently levels of performance.

Because culture is so misunderstood, many of the large-scale cultural change programmes that organisations undertake fail. The way to change culture is not by imposing a top-down set of bland values, but by improving understanding throughout the organisation of how culture works in practice; by helping leaders take responsibility for their own behaviours and to understand how they shape the culture in their teams.

If you have people you are responsible for, you are a leader and therefore the most important determinant of your team's culture. If your team and its members are to fulfil their potential, you must start with its culture. Creating a great culture is a leader's superpower.

People who understand this simple fact are immeasurably better placed to form high-performing teams than those who see culture as something beyond their control, immutable and unchangeable. Of course, unless you're the CEO, you cannot change the culture everywhere, but it's amazing what you can achieve almost immediately in your own team by taking a clear and action-oriented approach to creating an effective culture.

All effective cultures have the same seven characteristics

Culture is difficult to do well, but it is not complicated. Some organisations will boast about the power of their culture (and if they have a strong culture – fair enough). However, it is unlikely to be unique. It may have a distinct flavour of its own, but the reality is that all effective cultures share variations of the same seven characteristics. There is no need to spend millions of dollars on consultants. Simply do these seven things well:

- Discipline: we all do what we say we will do
- Support: we have each other's backs
- Trust: we assume our colleagues' positive intent
- Consistency: the rules apply to everybody
- Communication: there is space for all voices and we listen to each other
- Understanding: everybody understands what the culture is
- Prioritising: maintenance of the culture is a team priority

Developing understanding of these characteristics within your team requires little talent, but that doesn't mean it's easy. Nor is it something you can simply announce in a meeting and hope that everything will change. It won't. Building a great culture requires clarity and determined action. Great cultures rarely just happen. They are like beautiful but delicate plants, in need of continuous attention.

Cultures aren't a mystery; they are simply an amalgam of behaviours that determine how a team responds to events and seeks to achieve its goals. In strong cultures, these behaviours are more likely to be conscious and understood. Weak teams lack a clear understanding of how their behaviours shape their culture. A great example of why cultures matter, and how they enable us to perform at our best, comes from Daniel Pink in his book *Drive*.

Pink starts by identifying the factors that he believes enable us to thrive at work: autonomy, mastery and purpose.

Autonomy means the opportunity to do things our way.

Mastery means the development of our confidence and competence though training and feedback.

Purpose means the feeling that what we're doing matters and contributes to something bigger, whether for our colleagues, clients, company or wider society.

The closer we are able to get to autonomy, mastery and purpose, the more fulfilled and successful we will be.

The challenge most of us have is that the culture we work within is outside our control. Nevertheless, it is very important for us to be able to understand its characteristics and recognise the ways it influences our behaviours and emotions – as well as those around us. If you work in a large organisation, take the opportunity to observe cultures in other teams, or those of other organisations you come across. What are their relative attributes?

Observing the characteristics of different cultures and assessing them against my seven-point ideal is a great way to develop your understanding of how cultures work and how they affect us every day. You can begin to transform your team's performance right now by taking more active responsibility for shaping its culture.

Culture has a huge influence on our experience of work, job satisfaction and even our career progress. The more senior we are, the greater our opportunity to influence it. Our ability to build great cultures (and hence achieve great things) is founded on our understanding of what culture is and how a great culture is created.

Leadership: not just a skill, but *the* skill

Understanding leadership affords us a powerful foundation for our career success. It is difficult, but it is not complicated. The majority of us find ourselves responsible for others very early in our careers, and from that point on, our success is largely driven by our ability to turn those groups of disparate individuals into great teams. However, even before then, we can benefit enormously from understanding the principles of leadership.

Your watchwords should be clarity and action. No matter your position, experience, role or age, if you are the person in the room who is consistently clear and action-focused, you will quickly become somebody who everybody else always wants to have around.

CHAPTER 5

A Brief Story of Time

Time is the only resource we cannot replenish, yet so often we spend it badly – especially when it comes to our careers.

One of the biggest shocks I experienced on leaving the corporate world and starting my own business was the realisation of how much time in a typical working week is spent on autopilot. Even as a CEO. That's not the same as not working hard, but so much of what we do is performed without much conscious thought.

Think of all those times when you have dashed from a late train to try to make a meeting, swerving pedestrians in the drizzle, no time to grab a coffee. You make it just in time, mouth *sorry* as you squeeze in at the end of the table, wriggle out of your damp jacket and then sit through ninety minutes of pointless, ill-structured waffle.

Too much of work is like this: an end in itself rather than a conscious deployment of energy and time towards a clear goal. And to blame somebody else is to delude ourselves. It's our career – so if we want to get out what we put in, we need to use our most valuable resource to better effect.

Of course, we all need habits and routines to get through our day. We can't agonise over every tiny event. It's said that Barack

Obama and Steve Jobs would wear the same thing every day because it was just one less decision they had to make. But irrespective of what colour rollneck you choose, how often do you stop and ask if a meeting, project or presentation is really necessary? How often do you sit and deliberately allocate your time against the tasks that are most important?

Many of us sleepwalk through our days, and the more jammed our diaries become, the more we switch off our critical faculties and simply try to get through them. As the Red Queen said to Alice: we feel like we have to do all the running we can, just to stay in the same place.

We rely on habit because work is difficult, demanding and busy, but spending too much time on autopilot only makes things worse. We must, from time to time, switch it off. When we do, we'll discover that it is possible to work in a way that suits us better, enables us to progress more quickly and perhaps even work less hard.

The 20/80 rule

Most people at work use their time badly – even the most ambitious. The majority of people spend only about 20 per cent of their time on the projects that matter most. And consequently, in that 20 per cent achieve about 80 per cent of their most useful output. Twenty per cent is one day a week.

This might be why those organisations which have experimented with a four-day week have seen very little impact on productivity – because, in practice, many people are only working one effective day a week already. And the rest? It's all that stuff we do on autopilot, or is made up of the filler and guff organisations throw our way, stuff we have to wade through every week until we can find a little time to focus on what is actually going to make a difference. For most of us our working week is mostly filler – very little killer.

I'm not arguing that most people don't work hard. I'm arguing that so much of that hard work is wasted energy. This might not be primarily of our doing – organisations are very good at getting in their own way. But it is our problem. If we want to fulfil our ambitions, we have to spend our most valuable resource in a way that will give us maximum return.

An engineer defines efficiency as the ratio of useful output per unit input: for every unit of energy that you put in, how many do you get out? For an imaginary perpetual motion machine the ratio would be 1. In every real-world example, it is less than that. For example, a modern car that runs on petrol is about 35 per cent efficient, meaning 65 per cent of the money you spend on fuel goes to waste. Most of the missing energy is lost to heat either through the thermal inefficiency of the engine, the exhaust or friction. So the analogy is near perfect. A typical employee caught unthinkingly in the maw of their employer must put in a disproportionate amount of energy to achieve a useful output. The rest is lost in hot air.

The ROI of complaining

Before all those ambitious entrepreneurs and hot-shot start-ups get too smug, I've worked for them as well – and they are not immune. Autopilot is partly a function of organisational culture, but it is also a consequence of the human condition. Like so much else, we can sit around and blame everybody else, but nobody cares. Why should they, they've all got their own shit to deal with. There are few activities with a lower return-on-investment (ROI) than complaining. If we're going to get to where we want to be, we have to take control over how we spend our time.

What a difference it would make to our careers and the organisations we worked in if we spent 40 per cent of our time on the projects that really mattered (or, dare I say, 60 per cent). That's still only two to three days a week, but imagine what we could achieve.

Productivity misunderstood

There is a fetishisation of the subject of productivity in parts of the internet. Usually it seems to involve growing a beard, being filmed in moody shadows, getting up at 5.00 a.m. and taking cold showers. You can if you want.

In the context of work, productivity is usually explained as how we can organise ourselves and our lives to get more done in a given timeframe. But this is to fundamentally misunderstand the subject.

Our objective should not be to complete more tasks in a given time. It should be to achieve greater results in a given time. And these two things are not the same at all. Multitasking, far from being a sign of efficiency, is actually killing your productivity, perhaps even your private life. Without a proper plan, simply attempting to get more done will result in you increasing your input (time and energy) without meaningfully increasing your useful outputs – but, in order for the equation to balance, creating a lot more hot air.

The most productive and effective people are able to achieve better results through ruthless focus on the tasks that matter most. This should be your objective.

Inputs and outputs

If we're serious about our careers, we need to ask ourselves if the way we are spending our time is helping *us* achieve *our* personal goals, which (in simple terms) we can summarise as healthy, professional advancement. This is productivity.

We should not be focused on inputs – how many tasks we manage to get done in a given period – but rather outputs – how much of consequence to ourselves and our organisation we manage to complete. It is only the latter that counts.

At the end of the year, nobody will care how busy you've been (except perhaps your partner and kids). Your boss might nod sagely and thank you, but it's not going to move you forward in the competitive world of work. What will move you forward most quickly is your involvement in and completion of strategically significant tasks. These will be relatively few, but disproportionately important in terms of your internal profile and status. It is these that will make you indispensable.

The problem is if the working day is full of white noise it can be difficult to separate out the signal. And even if we manage to, how do we find the time and energy to do the priority projects well? Or do they just join the endless list of hurried tasks to be ticked off. This is a common, if not near-universal, experience.

One of the characteristics of the most successful people is not that they work harder (sure they work hard, but so do you). It's that they get a better ROI on that effort. And they do that by focusing their energies on the projects that move them and the team most rapidly towards their goal. This might sound cynical, but it's really not. It's an important truth everybody should understand. Successful people have the same number of hours in their days as everybody else – they just make better use of them than most.

And you can do it too.

1. If you don't know where you're going, you're never going to get there

You first need to be clear what your personal objectives are. These could be grand and hifalutin or more bitesize and short-term. Whatever works for you. But you need to have your own goals in mind when you consider how best to use your time. The greater the percentage of your time that is spent against tasks that will help you achieve your priorities, the more quickly you will achieve them. It stands to reason – and the failure to do so is why so often we don't.

2. Make the organisation's priorities your priorities

The most effective way for you to progress your career is to add value to the projects and tasks that matter most to the company. This might sound obvious, but it is quite unusual that people consciously do this. Every organisation has a lot of tasks it must perform adequately to function effectively, but only a very small number that will be the ultimate determinants of its future success. In my experience, even the most senior people often fail to effectively organise their time in this way, which is a common cause of leadership failure.

One of the surest ways to improve your time ROI is to understand the organisation's priorities and to be clear how you contribute towards them.

No matter your job title, you are ultimately employed to help the organisation, whatever it is, to achieve its goal. So often it's easy to get trapped into believing your tasks are an end in themselves. Despite how it may appear, they are not. Organisations value most the people who contribute most to the areas of greatest value.

In many roles, this is an effective way to become more productive. If you know what the organisation's number-one priority is, and you know how you are contributing towards it, then the tasks that contribute most directly to it should take up as much of your time and energy as possible. Ultimately, nobody will mind you cutting a load of 'filler' meetings if you are the person who is integral to all the biggest new-business wins. It's as straightforward as that.

Not only do most people not do this – thus missing out on an opportunity for competitive advantage – but most *organisations* are also bad at it. Typically, both employee and employer know what the most important tasks are, but lack the discipline to focus on them. The most effective people and the most effective organisations are crystal clear on what the priorities are, and deploy as much of their resources towards them as possible. If you try to do everything, you'll achieve nothing. Yet this is what so many people do. Which is why simply working harder is not the answer to achieving better results.

3. Every month: Zero-base your diary

At the start of every month, go through every recurring meeting and ask yourself:

- Is this necessary?
- Do I have to go?
- Have we got the right attendees?
- Do we use the time well?

Recurring meetings are some of the biggest time-sponges in our day. Even those that are important gradually become flabby, disorganised and ill-disciplined. As always, cut what you can – and where it's in your power, refresh stale meetings to keep them crisp, prompt and action-oriented.

4. Every week: Triage

Every Monday morning (or Friday afternoon or Sunday night, whenever suits you better), divide your tasks for the coming week into three categories:

⇒ *Urgent*

If a task takes less than five minutes to complete, do it immediately. Put an hour in your diary every Monday for these. Get them done – especially if they are unpleasant or stressful. If there are tasks that will take longer, but nevertheless are going to cause you distraction and stress the longer you leave them, get them done as early in the week as possible. Codie Sanchez, author of *Main Street Millionaire*, calls this eating the big frogs first, but the technique should also work for vegetarians.

⇒ *Priority projects*

Make sure you have the time and space to do a great job of the projects that will make the greatest difference to your personal progress. These may be relatively few, but their impact is significant. So clear your brain, clear your diary and preserve your energy for them. Where possible, do them at a time that suits you best so you are able to bring to them a clear head and maximum energy. Carve out time to do so.

⇒ *Cut, cut, cut!*

Cut as much as possible that doesn't fit into the two categories above. Use the time gained for priority projects or recovery.

5. Every day: One task, one cut

Every day, ask yourself these two simple questions:

- *'What single task is the most important thing I have to do well today?'*

  This might be related to your job, your family, your kids – whatever it is, make sure you have the time and energy to do that one thing well. It's good for your career, your private life, and your soul. Doing one important thing well every day is a win.

- *'What one thing can I cut today?'*
  There's always something. So cut it. And use the time for something that matters.

6. Every day of the week isn't the same

This is another of those statements that are so obvious they hardly need making. But it is also one of those obvious statements we pay almost no attention to when we plan our week. At different times of the week, our mood and energy fluctuate. There is a personal element to this, but there is also a general pattern that most of us feel.

Monday mornings tend to be low-energy, tetchy and sluggish, even more so in the winter (and in the UK that's the whole year except for a couple of weeks in August). Tuesday, Wednesday and Thursday are relatively productive and high-energy. And let's just admit it – not much gets done on Friday afternoons.

I once had a boss who insisted we held a town hall meeting every Monday morning at 9.00 a.m. It was horrendous. For everybody. He very generously 'delegated' responsibility to me, so for three Mondays out of four, I found myself standing in front of 250 people wondering what to say at a time when neither they nor I wanted to be there. It's an extreme example of a phenomenon that happens a lot. The time of week matters. If you have an important recurring meeting that you need people to be switched on for, do not have it on a Monday morning.

I'm sure gung-ho types will think I'm being ridiculous, but if you want to get stuff done and use your (and everybody else's) energy in as effective a way as possible, the 'when, where and who' all really matter.

7. Don't forget everybody else

Finally, everybody else. You should aspire not just to use your own time more effectively, but to help others do the same. I can remember the people I have worked with who did this, junior and senior, and such people are amazing to have in our lives. That can be you.

One of the most powerful ways is to simply be respectful of other people's time and energy. So:

- Don't be late
- Bring solutions not problems
- Ask people if they're okay
- Ask how you can help
- Accept that they're human too – so sometimes are going to do all the annoying things other humans do (breaking news: you do sometimes, too)

Don't just think you'd like to be this. Switch off the autopilot every now and again, and consciously be it. You can. Because like just about everything else in this book – it doesn't require talent. Only conscious thought and will.

Maximising your time ROI

To achieve career success and fulfilment we should strive to maximise the return we get from the hours we have available to us. Everybody has the same amount. What are you going to do with yours?

The clearer you are on what you want to achieve in the medium term, and the more focused you are able to be on the tasks that will get you there most quickly, the faster you will achieve your goal. So many of us are diligent, hard-working and conscientious, but get a poor return on our effort. Using your time well, and cutting as much as possible of the filler that clogs up your diary, isn't just a good habit – it will accelerate your career like little else.

CHAPTER 6

Communication: Simple, Precise and Concise

Communication is not simply an exchange of words; it is the bridge that connects individuals, builds relationships, resolves disagreements, aligns visions, and propels teams towards their objectives. It is how we understand others and how we ensure we're understood. A universal characteristic of great cultures, great teams and effective leaders is their ability to communicate well. The ability to communicate effectively, in a simple, precise and concise way, is one of the most useful skills you can learn.

The rise of email, social media, messengers and computers on every desk has led to an explosion in writing in the workplace. What was once a relatively rare and formal exercise, the writing and typing of a paper or memo for example, has now become a major feature of many people's working day. Unfortunately, if there has been a revolution in quantity of communication, there has been no such revolution in quality.

Because we talk, text and email from the minute we wake until the moment we sleep, we take for granted our ability to communicate. Yet we spend far too little time taking care to do it well. That an email has been sent doesn't guarantee it will be read, understood or acted upon, but if we want to increase our visibility, credibility and authority we need to make sure that ours are. The explosion of work-based communication has put a significant premium on the ability to follow the three principles that title this chapter: to make all of your communication simple, precise and concise.

Being able to communicate well matters and, as with any skill, we can improve with conscious practice. However, it's important to note that just doing something a lot doesn't necessarily make us better at it – indeed, it can ingrain bad habits that in the long run make us worse. Anybody who has tried to learn how to serve at tennis will understand this. Without *informed* practice, we do not improve.

Improvement at any skill requires effort, tuition and failure. We can all communicate well if we apply ourselves intelligently, just as we can all learn to serve (apparently). And that is an awful lot more difficult than writing a short, clear email. Or more bluntly, failure without learning is just failure.

This chapter is not about elegant prose or scintillating oratory. Neither are what's required, and both should be generally avoided when it comes to work. In the workplace, communication is about achieving your objective – so clarity and concision always trump the clever and verbose.

Imagine if every person and every organisation did just that.

Communication shapes how we are perceived by others – and, of course, how we in turn perceive those around us. Are we empathetic, abrupt, waffly, clear, timely, careless, diligent, quick, slow or slovenly? All can be inferred from how we behave in meetings, via email and when speaking. We know this because we draw these conclusions about others. However, here lies opportunity. Because so much corporate and work communication is of a poor quality, there is a significant competitive advantage in being able to do it well.

In order to improve your communication skills, there are six main categories you should be aware of and prioritise mastering.

1. Active listening

I once worked for somebody whose attitude towards listening was described as the 'silences while he waited to speak'. It was funny, because it was true – but in his defence, it is true of us all at times.

Active listening is the foundation of effective communication. It is how conversations, written or verbal, become meaningful exchanges of information. It's how we learn, how we develop understanding, how we show respect to others (and therefore gain respect ourselves) and is the basis of great decision-making. It is an intentional process; the pursuit of understanding. And we can all do it. It requires no learning or skill, but for the majority of us perhaps a little practice. Most of all, however, it requires that most precious and rare of commodities in the modern workplace: self-awareness.

Two ears; one mouth

The most important aspect of listening is the suspension of judgement. Anybody who has spent any time on social media knows how difficult this can be. Active listening requires us to pause our preconceptions and refrain from prematurely forming opinions while the speaker is still conveying their message (or even from the moment we read the subject line of the email). This deliberate delay in judgement allows for a better understanding of the other party's perspective, preventing misinterpretation, and is how you play your part in fostering an environment of open dialogue. For example, good networkers are good listeners – they ask questions and listen fully to the answers.

Often the people we would most benefit from listening a little more carefully to are those we most quickly rush to judge when they speak or write – the people we are in conflict with or are triggered by. You should make a particular effort to listen to those you disagree with. You don't have to agree with them, but it is important, if a resolution is to be found, that you understand them and that they feel heard. And, of course, it makes it far more likely that they will listen to you in return. Listening is a powerful sign of respect, and mutual respect is an important basis for finding solutions.

When we listen, we should use gestures and verbal cues to signal engagement. Nodding, maintaining eye contact, and offering affirming statements all convey to the speaker that their message is heard and valued, which in turn creates an atmosphere of trust and openness, encouraging the speaker to express themselves more freely. Active listeners ask insightful questions that are designed not to interrogate but to better understand the speaker's thoughts and feelings.

In the workplace, the significance of active listening is amplified. Team dynamics, project collaborations, and effective leadership all hinge on the ability of individuals to understand each other. By taking care to listen properly, we build stronger relationships with our colleagues and clients, we are better able to address their concerns, and we create a more inclusive environment where everyone feels heard and valued. The most common complaint I would hear from frustrated clients and customers was: *You're just not listening to me.*

Active listening sounds easy (excuse the pun!) but is more difficult than it seems – and the more stressed, triggered or pressured we feel, the harder it becomes to put into practice. The reality is that, at work, we feel one or more of those things quite often, so we must understand the value to ourselves of active listening just as much as we understand the value of speaking clearly and persuasively. Listening to others means they will be far more prepared to listen to us. And that should matter to you very much.

2. Precise

At various points through this book, I encourage you to write out your thoughts in advance of saying them out loud. This helps achieve two very important things: firstly, it clarifies your own ideas and, secondly, it helps you work out how to communicate them to others.

The process of sifting our thoughts and translating them into coherent ideas is not easy. Sometimes we will simply say what we're thinking out loud – a stream of consciousness that might help us, but does little for anybody else. This is our brain using words to try to organise our ideas. With a little time, we can shuffle them into an order that seems to make sense and, in some situations, this is perfectly acceptable. However, sometimes it's not – it makes us appear muddled, which in a way we are.

We've all sat in a meeting where somebody has begun to ask a question and several minutes later, they're still going. Everybody waits. What is the question? When will it arrive? There are false starts, dead-ends and various verbal re-works. Others begin to pick up their phones and check their messages. Eventually, when the speaker finally stops, the chair (if they're still paying attention) asks for clarification of what the question was.

There is no question, it's just somebody trying to work out what they think, out loud, in front of everybody else. All of us feel like this sometimes. But you'll notice that not everybody behaves like this. We learn that some people, when they speak, are worth paying attention to. Others less so. We all want to be the former.

Rather than using a verbalised stream of consciousness to organise your thoughts, write them down. It is a simple matter to work out on a pad what it is you think or want to say before you speak. If everybody were to do this, we might discover that the person with the rambling question had in fact a very important insight hidden in there somewhere – if they had only taken a little time to organise their thoughts.

Several years ago, I began to write a book on leadership. I didn't know how long it would be, or whether I had enough to say to fill even a chapter. I had a title and a collection of thoughts and feelings. I began to write these down.

Once you see words on a page, you discover they are different to how they sounded and felt when only in your head. In your head, you can feel an idea, but as you attempt to write it down it can drift from your grasp. You are forced to shuffle and refine the words to try to capture the true sentiment of your idea. Sometimes the words just flow, sometimes they never quite arrive; sometimes you read back what you've written and think that's just bullshit – and if you're not convinced, nobody else is going to be. My experience of writing is that at least 50 per cent of what initially seems like a good idea ends up in the bin. Thus, writing stuff down provides clarity for ourselves first of all.

Sometimes, ideas that appear crisp and clear in our heads can sound mushy, ill-formed and muddled when we try to put them into words. We know that because 'hard to put into words' is a phrase we often use. Ultimately, everything can be put into words, but sometimes it takes a little time and care to do so effectively. Writing out our ideas distils and edits. It helps to filter out the bad ones (most of them anyway) and sharpens the rest. Writing something out longhand is a great way to improve your thinking.

Just splurge it all out onto the page. It's only for you – you don't need to worry about punctuation or spelling or any of the rest. Just get it out. Then read it back. I guarantee you'll be able to improve on it: make it shorter, sharper or tighter or easier to explain. Because remember, that is the point: you're improving your ability to communicate it to others. At work, an idea that stays only in your head is like the tree that falls in an empty forest. If nobody else understands your idea, does it even exist?

Don't be the person asking long, waffly semi-questions. If in doubt – write them out. It'll take thirty seconds and might save five minutes, as well as making you look smart. And who doesn't want that? Smart questions signal smart people.

3. Simple

Ernest Hemingway was one of the greatest and most influential writers of the twentieth century. Part of his genius was the ability to convey a vivid sense of place with simple language and minimal description. His writing employs no unnecessary embellishments or lengthy descriptions, yet we instantly inhabit the world he creates. I defy you to finish the following short extract and refrain from flicking away flies while sitting on the dusty station steps.

> *The hills across the valley of the Ebro were long and white. On this side there was no shade and no trees and the station was between two lines of rails in the sun. Close against the side of the station there was the warm shadow of the building and a curtain, made of strings of bamboo beads, hung across the open door into the bar, to keep out flies. The American and the girl with him sat at a table in the shade, outside the building. It was very hot and the express from Barcelona would come in forty minutes.*
>
> 'Hills Like White Elephants', Ernest Hemingway

Every word is unremarkable, yet the effect of the whole quite remarkable.

Hemingway may seem an unnecessarily high bar to set when

considering how to write better emails, but there is a practical point. If a novelist of his renown can evoke such powerful emotions with simple, everyday language, then it is not the words, grammar and punctuation that we need to know, but how to use them.

A word to pronounce with care

Cant is one of my favourite words.

Cant – definition

noun

- Insincere or hypocritical language, especially that used by people in positions of authority or power.

For example: He spoke with such cant that it was hard to believe anything he said.

- A specialised vocabulary or set of expressions used within a particular group or profession.

For example: The jargon of the [. . .] profession is full of cant.*

*Insert the name of your industry here.

There is a fetish in businesses of all types for acronyms, buzz-words and other assorted bullshit. This cant is used to exclude and obscure. It excludes those not in the profession through the use of unfamiliar terms. And it obscures even for those within the profession, through impenetrable language. Sometimes it is deliberate, sometimes not. But it is almost always unnecessary.

A very everyday example is acronyms. Businesses love acronyms. Many is the meeting that I've sat through listening to a speaker who is using consonants and vowels more frequently than words. *What do they all mean?* I've wondered to myself. Not wanting to appear ignorant, I've stayed silent, glancing furtively at the poker faces about me.

The longer you leave it, the harder it is to speak up, yet the more confused you become. At length, somebody, in desperation, asks. There's an audible sigh from the room, not of frustration, but relief.

There is a perception among some that making things sound complicated and using long words are signs of intelligence and competence. I offer Hemingway as proof of the opposite. You might claim that his writing is not comparable to that of more technical fields. If so, I would direct you to one of the greatest physicists of the twentieth century, Richard Feynman, whose lectures on everything from particle physics to general relativity are not just astonishing in their accessibility, but genuinely entertaining (and easy to find on YouTube).

The ability to explain the complicated in simple terms is the ultimate sign of comprehension and mastery of a subject – not the use of long words and jargon. It is a powerful thing to possess the understanding and confidence to speak and write simply when all about you are doing the opposite.

A good rule of thumb when writing, or speaking to an audience, is to follow the principles employed by the originators of the Oxford English Dictionary. Dictionaries make definitions of complicated or nuanced entries understandable to a wide audience through ensuring that only common words are used in their explanations. If you've ever tried to explain the meaning of a word to somebody, even a very common word, you'll know this is not an easy thing to do. A lexicographer's objectives are clarity and accessibility. The anti-cant, so to speak. Yours should be too. It's not always easy, but in search of cut-through, comprehension and retention of your ideas, it is worth the effort to say it simply.

4. Concise

Being concise is having the ability to express yourself succinctly without sacrificing the most relevant and important information. Cut too much and you lose meaning, too little and you lose your audience. A concise message respects the recipient's time and, in business, enhances the likelihood of its key points being retained and acted upon.

Being concise requires you to identify and prioritise the most important elements of your message. This is particularly pertinent in written communication, where clarity and brevity often go hand in hand, but the same applies to the spoken word. In communication, there is an inverse relationship between the length of a message and how much of it people are able to absorb.

In today's workplace, with multiple communication channels available to us, attention spans fleeting and demands on our time growing, the value of concision is further amplified. If we want our communication to be as effective as possible, we must do the work so our audience doesn't have to. For example, voice notes may be convenient for you, but if you want the recipient to listen to them – keep them short. And if you really care – write them out.

Concise communication mitigates the risk of misunderstandings, reduces the likelihood of information overload, and enhances the overall efficiency of organisational processes. The use of simple language and construction wherever possible (which is not the same as dumbed-down or simplistic language) speeds comprehension even for a technical audience familiar with the topic. It's not always easy to do, but there is clear benefit in making the effort. As the Roman orator Cicero is supposed to have said: 'If I'd have had more time, I'd have written a shorter letter.' Writing, as they say, is re-writing.

Most important of all for you, the cumulative effect of being concise is to increase the chances of what you write being retained and what you say being remembered.

5. Non-verbal communication

Body language plays an important role in conveying emotion and intention, as well as influencing how we perceive others and how they perceive us. It encompasses a broad spectrum of non-verbal signals, including facial expressions, gestures, posture, eye contact, and even the tone and pitch of our voice. These cues operate as an unspoken dialogue, providing context and depth to spoken words. They can also reveal feelings we would prefer remained hidden.

The challenge with body language is that it is usually something we are unaware of ourselves, even as we subconsciously read the non-verbal cues of others. What complicates matters further is that, like any language, it is open to misinterpretation – it can be an unreliable ally. We may confuse shyness for arrogance, uncertainty for stubbornness, nervousness for flippancy. And others may make the same mistakes when they observe us. Nevertheless, in the workplace, perceptions matter a great deal and we should be aware of and consider how we appear to others – particularly in moments of stress and pressure, when our non-verbal signals might be most acute.

It's not something we should obsess about, but it is something we should be aware of when speaking, when listening to others and when considering how we wish to be perceived. Consider the following:

- Posture: The way we carry ourselves can convey confidence, openness or authority. Slouched shoulders may be read by others as disinterest or fatigue.

- Facial expressions: The face is a canvas of emotions to which we are finely attuned, capable of wordlessly conveying elation, sorrow, surprise or rage. A smile really can warm a room, a furrowed brow set nerves jangling.
- Eye contact: Eyes are powerful communicators, and the level of eye contact during a conversation can convey a range of emotions and intentions. Direct eye contact is often associated with honesty, sincerity and engagement, while avoiding eye contact may be interpreted as discomfort or dishonesty. However, striking the right balance is crucial to fostering trust and connection. Too much is unsettling, too little can be interpreted as shifty or dishonest.
- Tone and pitch of voice: Non-verbal cues extend beyond the realm of body language to include the tone and pitch of our voice. A warm, even tone can convey empathy and understanding, while a sharp or high-pitched tone may indicate stress, anger or tension. Effective communication requires aligning verbal and non-verbal elements to ensure a consistent and authentic message.

Taking care to understanding the importance of the non-verbal when interacting face-to-face, when presenting, or when on-screen, can have a significant impact on the power and effectiveness of your delivery. The above principles are not complicated – indeed, many are instinctive – but sometimes we need to understand them in order to master them. We may feel uncertain, but we do not want it to show; we may be elated but need to commiserate; angry but need to be emollient. Our words matter, but so do our actions.

When presenting, you should stand up straight, not slouch. You should not put your hands in your pockets. You should make eye contact with the audience, deliberately allowing your gaze to shift from front to back and side to side. If you're on a platform, you should move around a little to avoid appearing frozen. This is all obvious, but many people don't do it. If you are new to presenting, ask for feedback to understand how you came across. Very often these are easy fixes that make a huge difference.

A common mistake is to present only to the person you subconsciously perceive to be the most important or most senior in the room. Not only does this rapidly become apparent to the rest of the attendees, it is also very uncomfortable for the person concerned.

I was once a member of a team presenting to a large group of very important clients. Our boss, a distant and aloof figure, had been absent for all but the final meeting, confident he needed no practice or preparation. He delivered a large chunk of the presentation reasonably well, but spoke throughout fixedly towards a single person seated on the front row, believing them to be the most senior and important client. Only on shaking his hand at the meeting's conclusion did he discover the individual was a member of our own team.

And thus, for the want of a nail, the kingdom was lost.

There is also some evidence that while our mood influences our behaviours (for example, if we feel nervous, we appear nervous), the reverse can also be true. For instance, if we adopt a confident or relaxed manner, it may make us feel more relaxed. I'm not arguing for doing Superman poses in front of the bathroom mirror (though if that works for you, keep doing it), but I do believe that a confident manner can create a positive mindset, and that positive behaviours can engender positive feelings. It is reasonable to argue that if we consciously adopt a warm, welcoming and confident manner, then those we are with are more likely to mirror our behaviour. Similarly, if we appear worried, those we are with will worry too.

Non-verbal cues matter, but our senses can betray us

However, we should beware. Our senses are not always reliable, and we often misinterpret the non-verbal cues of others. Different cultural backgrounds, individual personalities and contextual factors all have a significant influence on both the meaning of body language and the conclusions we draw from it. I've often come out of meetings and only discovered afterwards, in discussion with colleagues, that they had read the feelings of other attendees completely differently to how I had.

This doesn't mean we should disregard our senses, but rather that we should understand they are only one component of how we communicate, adding depth and authenticity to our words. In studying others, their body language gives us cues and clues, not whole sentences. The surest way, as always, is to seek verbal clarification to avoid misunderstandings.

And smile warmly while you're doing it.

6. And finally: getting the most out of email

The tyranny of the magic porridge pot inbox is one of the great scourges of modern working life. Despite the rise of platforms such as Slack and Teams, there is little evidence of a reduction in email volume. This overload means we must necessarily cut corners. We cannot read, digest and reply to all the messages we receive, at least not if we wish to ever do anything else. This is why being precise and concise matters so much – we want our messages to be the ones that are read, understood and responded to.

Furthermore, email lasts for ever, can be endlessly forwarded and clumsy mistakes are easy to make. Therefore, though the rules that follow might seem like common sense, if you look through your inbox after reading them, I guarantee that you will find plenty of examples where an application of those same principles would have been a very good idea indeed. It's another easy win, as well as a common pitfall avoided.

Do:

- *Use a clear subject line*
  Always include a concise and informative subject line that clearly conveys the purpose of the email. This helps recipients understand the content at a glance and assess its relative importance.
- *Be brief*
  Get to the point quickly and use simple, precise and concise language. Long-winded emails may not get the attention they require.
- *Prioritise the contents*
  Always include the most important information at the start.
- *Be mindful of tone*
  Always use a professional and courteous tone no matter how tempting it is sometimes to do otherwise. Emails last for ever.
- *Always proofread*
  Review your email for typos and grammatical errors before sending. This is easier than ever with modern software. A polished email reflects positively on you. A careless one, poorly.

- *Use bullet points*
  In longer emails, use labelled bullet points to make your email quick to read and easy to digest. Breaking up large chunks of text enhances comprehension and helps the recipient absorb information more effectively.

- *Respond promptly*
  This is easier said than done, but it certainly applies to important emails. Even if you cannot provide a complete response immediately, acknowledge receipt and set expectations for when you will be able to send a more complete response.

- *Use a professional signature*
  Many companies will provide this automatically, but ensure your details are correct. You should include your full name, company name, job title and website as a minimum.

- *Summarise long mails*
  If it has to be a long email or has a long attachment you wish the recipients to read, consider including a short bullet-pointed management summary to make their lives easier.

Don't:

- *Use vague subject lines*
  If you want people to prioritise reading and responding to your mails, avoid generic or vague subject lines. For example, the perennial favourite: 'Update'.

- *Overuse emojis and abbreviations*
  Don't overuse emojis, abbreviations or informal language. Keep the tone professional.

- *'Reply All' or cc everybody unnecessarily*
  Much that clogs up our inboxes is unnecessary use of cc's and 'Reply All'. Don't use 'Reply All' unless you are sure everyone needs to see your response. They usually do not.

- *Never send sensitive information unencrypted*
  Don't send sensitive or confidential information without encrypting it, especially if it involves personal or financial details. Protecting privacy is crucial in professional communication – and crucial in protecting your own professional reputation.

- *Never email when angry*
  Never reply immediately to an email that has triggered you. Leave it until you have calmed down, then take a considered view on your response – indeed whether to respond by email at all. If you find yourself hammering out an angry reply, put it in your drafts for an hour or two. I guarantee you will tone it down (or even delete it) once you've calmed down.

- *Never email after drinking*
  This might sound funny, but it happens and can shred reputations.

- *Never use intemperate language*
  Always be professional in an email. If at all possible, never write anything in an email that you would not wish to be made public. Never speak badly of a colleague or client on email unless it is unavoidable. All company emails are retained on the company's servers and in most jurisdictions your employer, other employees and even third parties retain a legal right to see them. For ever!

- *Don't rely solely on email if it's very urgent or important*
  If a quick response is needed, consider using alternative communication methods such as phone calls or instant messaging. Or even – shock, horror – face-to-face.

Communication: a career-long skill that you'll use every day

Effective communication is key to becoming indispensable in the workplace. It transcends job roles and industries, enabling you to navigate complex work environments, build strong relationships and contribute meaningfully to organisational goals – even from a very junior position.

The ability to articulate a vision, motivate your team and manage your stakeholders (bosses and customers, for example) will be shaped by the precise, concise and uncomplicated nature of your communication. It can be the difference between being trusted and respected – and not.

Conflict is an inevitable – perhaps even necessary – part of the workplace. Effective communication is needed to ensure that all voices are heard, ideas torture-tested, grievances aired and solutions found. Effective communicators are able to passionately disagree without being disrespectful or falling out.

Whether with colleagues, clients, customers or superiors, the ability to communicate well will set you apart, demonstrating the value not just of your ideas, but your value as a thoughtful, insightful and professional team member.

CHAPTER 7

Stuck in the Middle With You

I once spoke at a leadership development programme for a select group of hand-picked, 'Next Generation Leaders' who worked for a large car manufacturer. The day finished and it seemed to have gone very well. There was high engagement, lots of great questions, and plenty of energy and suggested actions afterwards. I left feeling very pleased with myself.

A week later, I found myself in a meeting with one of their bosses. We got talking about the programme. Without thinking I remarked, 'It's amazing how often, no matter who's in the audience, the most common bit of feedback I get is: I wish my boss had done this course instead of me.'

The moment I said it I saw the look on her face. We shared an awkward laugh.

'None of our lot I hope?'

They were an important client and I'm a coward.

'No,' I lied, 'interestingly, none of yours did.'

It is, without question, the most common piece of feedback I get.

Learning from the middle

'What should I do,' I'm asked, 'if I agree with all this stuff about how to run great meetings and how to be a great team member and how to understand leadership; I learn how to be an effective communicator, but I'm stuck in a culture and with a boss who just doesn't get any of it?' (This is a rather more polite version of how the question is usually asked.)

Throughout our careers, we find ourselves working with all sorts of different people and, even if you feel well led and respected right now, there will have been times in the past, or there are likely to be times in the future, where you don't. You'd be an unusual and fortunate person were this not the case.

For the majority of our careers, most of us find ourselves simultaneously in the position of team leader and team member; being a boss and having a boss. To succeed, we need to be good for the careers of the people we are responsible for *and* the people we are responsible to. Furthermore, though we are responsible for the culture and effectiveness of our teams, we have to achieve this within the context of the wider organisation. We are far from powerless over how we work and the direction of our careers, but we rarely find ourselves masters of all we survey.

Liking your boss isn't a reliable guide to whether they're a good leader or not. You can like them very much and they can be useless, or you could not 'click' with them at all and they could be a very effective leader. Regardless, there are strategies you can employ that will enable you to survive, even thrive, in a difficult environment. In fact, you may be surprised at what's possible when you're clear on your goals and organised about how to achieve them. In this chapter, we will explore strategies you can employ when it's just not quite working out with your boss.

It's something we're all likely to experience at some point, so here's my seven-step survival guide in case it happens to you.

1. Understanding is the prelude to solving

Just as all parents moan, from time-to-time, about their kids' school, so everybody enjoys an occasional moan about their boss. And, sorry to break it to you, but your boss probably also occasionally moans about you. None of which means it's necessarily a bad school, that your boss is a bad leader, or that they don't rate you. Sometimes it's just how we let off steam and bond with our peers, friends and colleagues.

Yet the quality of the relationship we have with our boss matters a great deal. It can determine our rate of career progress, happiness, job satisfaction, pay – even our mental health. Many of us spend more time with work colleagues than our families, and the organising principle for this book is to ensure you get an appropriate return from that level of time investment. More importantly, great leaders beget great leaders – so if you are lucky enough to have an effective and successful boss, you want to make sure you gain as much as possible from their experience and support. If they're average, and by definition of course most will be, you can still learn from them – you just need a clear head and a good plan. And if they're a disaster . . . well, we'll come to that.

I've had good bosses and bad bosses. Bosses I've liked and some not. However, with the gift of hindsight, I can see that the two do not correlate very closely. The one who stood screaming on the Arne Jacobsen chair in his plush office, before throwing his pencil at me and telling me to f**k off, was objectively useless – something I think both of us already knew. The one who called me a f**king c**t in the middle of a crowded room I ended up respecting very much and they ultimately became a good friend (not least as a consequence of that rather unfortunate spat). The one who initially I admired and liked the most, it transpired, was a psychopath.

Understanding is always the prelude to solving, so take a moment to reflect. Start at the start. How can you evaluate your boss with some degree of objectivity? How are they really doing? Not in an idealised version of the world, but against the actual challenges they face. For example, what is their boss like – no small consideration when seeking to understanding their behaviour. It's easy to moan about the bad stuff, but what do they do well? How could they do better? Do you believe others (people you know or have worked with before, for example) could do better in their situation? Could you . . . ?

The purpose of this exercise is to force you to be realistic – to move from moaning to understanding – even, dare I suggest, empathising. This is important because although moaning might briefly make you feel better, it can become a habit that consumes you. All leadership is difficult, all leaders make mistakes.

When attempting to improve our relationship with our boss, we should ask ourselves many of the same questions we might ask ourselves of our team:

- What are you getting from them that you most value?
- What is it you want from them that you aren't getting and why?
- Do others appear to have a more effective relationship with them than you do – and why?
- Are there things you could do (or stop doing) that could improve this situation?
- What is your boss best at?

- What are their greatest strengths?
- Have you discussed any of this with them?

Take these questions seriously and challenge yourself to be objective. Even with bosses I once held in low regard, I now believe that in my frustration, perhaps arrogance, I allowed their flaws to obscure their strengths. And conveniently ignored my own weaknesses – of which there are plenty. Many were more effective than I believed at the time, and they certainly had strengths I did not. Looking back, there is much more I could have learned from them than I allowed myself to believe. I also could and should have done a better job of addressing the issues I had with them. It takes two to tango.

2. Is it you or is it them? (Or is it money?)

If your relationship with your boss is poor, it is very easy to lay the blame exclusively at their door. Not only is this often not the case, but to believe so is to deny yourself agency. Blaming them is easy, but also disempowering. Sometimes it's easier to blame somebody else than ask awkward questions of yourself. Don't allow yourself to default to making your issues all about your boss and your perception of their flaws. How much of what frustrates you is really their fault? How much of it is yours – and how much is just an unavoidable consequence of circumstance? We're very good at seeing all the things other people get wrong, yet none of us are without our faults and flaws. Furthermore, a meeting to discuss all that's wrong with your boss is a highly ill-advised path to take. It is far more productive to begin with yourself. After all, you can control you.

What is it that you . . .

- want?
- need?
- aspire to?
- are worried by?
- don't understand?
- would like to do more of?
- feel you aren't being recognised for?
- would like to be trained to do?
- would like to be promoted to?
- would like to be considered for?

All of these are perfectly reasonable bases for conversations with your boss – and needn't be in any way confrontational. You may or may not like the answers, but these questions are a good place to start.

Finally, let's acknowledge the elephant in the room.

Irrespective of what Harvard Business School case studies repeatedly claim, salary can be a major source of resentment. Different cultures around the world have different comfort levels around discussing pay – as do different people within them. In my experience, when it comes to pay (and much else besides), the squeaky wheel gets the oil, so if your real issue is money then you have to be honest (yes, that word again) with yourself first. Don't kid yourself that this is a clash of values and behaviours when in reality it's about money. If it's money that's really bugging you, then you have to say it. Don't make them guess, because – intentionally or not – they won't.

3. Don't assume your boss knows what you're thinking

Perhaps they do, perhaps they don't. Unless you talk to them, you'll never know.

You might feel your boss just ought to know – that it's their job. Well . . . maybe. But it's you that's pissed off and frustrated and missing out, not them. So, whatever you feel about the situation, it's in your interest to talk to them about it.

Empathy is a valuable attribute of a leader, but if you want to achieve your own goals you also need to be empathetic towards your boss. Empathy doesn't mean being soft and cuddly; it is being able to understand and share the emotions of another. It is very helpful to spend a moment thinking about this before important or difficult conversations; not moaning about the other party's lack of empathy, but assessing your own.

How does your boss feel? Are they stressed, happy, unhappy, over-worked, worried about impending change? Don't underestimate the extent to which their relationship with their own boss may influence their relationship with you.

Be realistic. Do they see you as a potential ally or a problem to be solved? They also are human, so are likely to feel all the emotions you feel at one time or another. Many people in leadership positions are young, inexperienced and have received little training for their role. I remember some of my early bosses who at the time seemed so old and experienced, but who now I can see had only a fraction more experience than I had at the time; young people who were also struggling to keep their heads above water. How much more we could have achieved together had I tried harder to be an ally rather than a needy fledgling.

The better able you are to put yourself in your boss's shoes, the more likely you are to build an effective relationship with them and ensure you get what you want and need from it.

4. Consider your career ROI

What's in it for you?

Maybe to some people, this question feels a little aggressive or even mercenary. It's not supposed to – it's an important question to ask yourself from time to time, irrespective of your relationship with your employer. Indeed, perhaps it is even more important if you have a boss with whom you have a great relationship. We all have our own ambitions and, unless we keep a careful eye on them, it's possible to spend a lot of time doing a great job for other people and not get the personal benefits that we seek or deserve.

Your desired rate of return is something only you can decide. There are the obvious measures, such as pay and promotion, but I also mean: are you learning enough, being stretched enough, being supported enough, being told things you might not want to hear enough? Are you in or out of your comfort zone enough (an important component in how we learn and progress)? Do you feel fulfilled often enough?

Even the most apparently meteoric careers aren't straight lines. People who manage their careers well find a good balance between how they deliver an ROI to their employer and how their employer delivers an ROI to them.

Irrespective of how you feel on a personal level about your boss, you should ask yourself whether they are helping you get closer to where you want to be. Are there ways that you can help each other more? I have worked for people who I really didn't like, but who I learned positive lessons from that I credit them for and remember to this day. Similarly, one of the most painful but greatest periods of learning in my career came when enduring the failure of my bosses and myself.

I'm not telling you to suck it up, but I *am* asking: what's in it for you? You might discover that there is much that makes a degree of discomfort worthwhile* – at least for a period.

*Disclaimer. That said, you may conclude the opposite. You could (perfectly reasonably) conclude that life is too short to work for people who you really don't like, no matter how much you're paid or how much you learn. In which case – don't.

5. Have the difficult conversations

By definition, we all find them uncomfortable – if we didn't, then they'd just be conversations. But there's no doubt that some of the conversations we find most uncomfortable and challenging are the most important we will have in our careers. So don't dodge them.

Career roadblocks and speedbumps occur all the time. Sometimes you can manoeuvre around them; sometimes a perfectly effective strategy is to ignore them and see if the problem goes away. Despite my urging you to action, you'd be surprised how effective this can be on occasion – just don't rely on it too often. However, sometimes, in order to keep moving forward, you've got to get out of the car, get the rip-proof gloves on, pick up the chainsaw and start dragging logs out of the way.

I only have three rules for difficult conversations:

⇒ *Prepare properly*

Effective preparation is the secret sauce to so much of what makes for a successful career. Too many people under-prepare and consequently under-perform in a whole range of situations, from presentations to pay negotiations. If you want to show up at your best – prepare properly.

Once you're clear on the points you want to make, write them down – it will clarify your thinking. Distil your ideas into bullet points, and don't have too many – three is usually optimum, five an absolute maximum. If necessary, take this list into the conversation with you either as a handwritten aide memoire in your daybook or a skeleton agenda which you share (a judgement call that will depend on circumstances).

Under pressure, it's easy to forget, to fumble or just lose your nerve. Writing down the points you want to make will help you make them more clearly.

⇒ *Be clear on your objective*

Be clear with yourself about what you want to achieve. Having been a CEO for many years, I often found myself having to help the other party work out what it was they were trying to say or what they wanted. (Hint: it very often turned out to be more money.) If you're not clear, there's no way the other person will be. If necessary, write this down too.

A common mistake people make is to squeeze in the topic that they most want to discuss as a postscript to a meeting ostensibly about something else altogether. We've all done it. Sometimes this might be a necessary subterfuge, but mostly it isn't. The main problem with this approach is that you are inevitably out of time just as you need it most.

Put what matters most first. The rest can wait. Clarity does not guarantee success, but it is the only way you have a chance of getting what you want.

⇒ *Just f**king do it*

This is far and away the best advice I can give regarding difficult conversations. Get your shit together beforehand and just do it. If you wait for the right time, I guarantee it'll never come. We worry about exactly how to begin, or how to structure the meeting, yet the best way, by far, is to just start. This is not flippant, it's true.

Nobody will remember how you began – what matters is how the meeting concludes. Once you get started, you'll be amazed at how often conversations that had filled you with dread turn out to be not that difficult after all. But to get there – you've got to get going.

6. Invest in the relationship

Sometimes I hear people talk about their relationship with their boss and I can't help but end up feeling sorry not for them, but their boss.

A relationship with your boss is like any other. No matter their strengths and weaknesses, you will only get out as much as you put in. So, before you decide everything is their fault, spend a moment asking yourself the following questions:

- Are your expectations of them realistic?
- Are your expectations of yourself realistic?
- How clear have you been with them to this point?
- Is it possible that they are saying things to you that you're just not hearing, or don't want to hear?
- Have you always kept your side of any agreement between you?

If not, it is unreasonable to be frustrated with them for doing the same – it might even be that they are mirroring you.

If they feel you are not acting in good faith towards them, then they will be understandably frustrated with you – or worse. Trust is a two-way street.

And, if you're serious about finding a solution, then make sure you do the following:

- Take responsibility for your own mistakes and flaws – or times when you haven't been easy to work with.
- Accept that building relationships, and especially re-building poor relationships, is a process. One meeting won't solve all your frustrations.
- Be yourself, be honest and be reasonable.
- Most important of all: Actions speak louder than words. What you do and how you behave counts for far more in sustaining an effective relationship than what you say.

7. What to do if nothing works

If the relationship with your boss is not working for you, your starting point must be to have a strategy to try to improve it. You should not let a poor working relationship fester. Not only will it make you miserable, it will hold you back. All relationships have two parties and you have to start by playing your part as well as you can. The objective is not to be friends with your colleagues; it is to have a fulfilling and successful career.

The steps listed above may make resolution seem like a long and daunting process but, in my experience, it is amazing how often one (not very) difficult conversation can transform a relationship. Most people want things to work. Most people don't want conflict, and value you taking the time to be honest and clear with them about your ambitions or frustrations.

That all said, sometimes it just doesn't work out. Despite your best efforts, the relationship with your boss might remain broken. In this case you have three choices.

1. Put your head down and keep buggering on. Maybe things will get better. Maybe.

2. You don't like it, but you can see very clearly why putting up with the situation is in your best interests. If you choose this approach, make sure you are clear what's in it for you, and set yourself realistic timeframes and goals. If you cannot, then this is just number one with added self-delusion.

3. Leave. For most people who've worked their way through my list and got nowhere, this is the right thing to do. It shouldn't be your first choice, but if you're serious about getting to where you want to go, learning what you need, and growing in the ways you want to grow, then sometimes that boss is bad for you. Ultimately, some bosses are just not much good – or, more charitably, you're mutually incompatible. So get out.

A final caveat and word of warning

If you're frustrated with your boss, or with your working environment, you should begin with the attitude that the onus to make it work lies at least as much with you as with the other party. You may not think this fair, but it's in your interests to fix the problem, so taking the initiative is common sense.

It's surprising how often people find it easier to leave a role than simply tell their boss of their frustrations. Of course, your boss should know. And if they were doing their job properly, they would ask. But that's just not how the world works sometimes. To get what you want from your career, and all those hours you spend at work, you need to be clear, you need a plan and you need to take responsibility. Don't cut off your nose to spite your face.

It's a cliché that the best time to get a great new job is when you're happy and content in the one you have, and there's some truth to that. True or not, life doesn't usually come at you in such a convenient and comfortable way. Changing jobs because you're frustrated or unhappy is a perfectly rational thing to do, but beware the distress purchase. Don't simply jump from the frying pan into the fire.

If this is your decision, then you should follow the principles I lay out in this book: be clear and honest (with yourself) about the problem you are trying to solve and explicit about what you want from your next role.

This, however, is one of those occasions where I would advise you to take your time.

Stuck in the Middle With You (part 2)

or

What Do Your Team Say About You?

Before going any further, you need to complete a very important exercise.

Go back to the start of the preceding chapter and wherever the word 'boss' appears, replace it with your own name and make the protagonist somebody in your team. Perhaps try it with several different people.

How do you score yourself? What are you going to do about it?

CHAPTER 8

Promotion and Pay

Nobody cares about your career as much as you, not least because everybody else is too busy worrying about their own. Throughout your career, you are its only constant and its most invested supporter. This doesn't mean that nobody else cares, far from it, but it does mean that you cannot simply take progress for granted. To progress, you need a plan. And, as always, a plan comes in two parts: clarity and action.

With regards to career advancement, clarity represents an understanding of your personal goals, and a hypothesis of how you will achieve them. It is difficult to plan our careers in detail many years in advance, but long-term ambition is a useful signpost for the decisions you take today.

However, the nature of work means we must think both long and short term. I have worked with many ambitious people who are so focused on the next job that they forget about the current one – and are consequently left behind. Nobody gets promoted if they aren't doing a good job in their current role, regardless of how ambitious they are. It is useful to think ahead, but your most important job is the one you have right now.

A sense of personal progress is critical at all stages of our careers.

It is possible to put up with all kinds of difficulties if we believe we are getting a return for the energy (and perhaps blood, sweat and tears) we are expending. One of the main reasons for career disillusion, even burnout, is when people feel they are not getting that.

Even if you are not clear on precisely where you would like your career to take you, forward progress through the accumulation of skills and experience can be an end in itself. The more you progress and learn, the greater the number of opportunities that will open up for you, and ultimately it is opportunities rather than a single destination that you should aspire to.

The more successful you are, the more numerous your opportunities and the greater control you will have over your future direction. Indispensable people may be irreplaceable to their employer, but their employer is not irreplaceable to them.

If you're going to do something that takes up as much of your time as work does, you should try to do it well, and be appropriately rewarded for doing so. Progress is a very personal thing; it means different things to different people and not everything at work is about pay rises and promotions. There are myriad reasons we choose to do what we do but, whatever progress means to you at this moment, you need a plan to make it happen – you cannot just rely on all the pieces simply falling into place.

Musical chairs

Organisational structures are commonly described as a pyramid: wide at the bottom, narrow at the top. It's a reasonably accurate model and one we are familiar with, but we often don't think about its implications for ourselves. What it means in practice is that a career can be seen rather like a game of musical chairs.

Those who have young children will know that for a seemingly innocent parlour game musical chairs can be rather intense. At the beginning, there are thirty or so children all sitting in the middle of the room. On comes Taylor Swift, up they all stand chatting and laughing, and around they go. At first there is relative calm – there are lots of children, but also lots of chairs. A parent with a handful of chocolate cake takes away a chair, the music stops. Twenty-nine of the children easily find a seat. One child, after only a small and easily resolved scuffle, loses out.

For a few rounds this pattern continues; the odds are in the children's favour, finding a chair is relatively easy. However, the inexorable logic of probability gradually turns the screw. With ten children remaining, each has a ten per cent chance of losing out. Tempers begin to fray; parental intervention becomes more necessary. By the time there are four children and three chairs, the odds have dramatically worsened. At one chair, it always ends in a sugar-fuelled fight.

We like to think that we are not in competition with our colleagues, but the reality is: we are. At each step up in our career, there exists an imbalance between candidates and opportunities. At each step up, a chair is taken away.

Initially, this imbalance is so small as to be inconsequential. At first, everybody gets promoted eventually. It might be frustrating if you have to wait six months longer than a colleague, but the opportunity will come. However, in time, the number of opportunities for advancement lessen, the rewards for promotion become more noticeable and the candidate pool, though smaller in absolute terms, remains large. The rewards improve, but the odds worsen.

This is not some grim argument in favour of the survival of the fittest. However, in order to progress through your career, you cannot simply rely on the music happening to stop just as you pass the empty chair. This can happen – being in the right place at the right time is a skill (if that's the right word) that has helped many a career. But you cannot depend upon it. If you want the next role, you are in competition for it and you need to make sure you've made your case. Does that guarantee success? No, but it will improve your chances.

If you don't ask, you don't get

This could have been the title of this chapter.

Promotions help you improve the quality of your life, provide you with a greater sense of accomplishment, allow you to take more control over how you work, offer new experiences to learn and increase the range of future opportunities available to you. And, of course, you get paid more.

But for every promotion, pay rise or job you get, somebody else misses out. And vice versa; if somebody else gets it, then you don't. The competitive nature of career progression means that simply waiting and hoping that all you deserve will in time come your way is not a reliable approach. If you want to progress, you have to know what you want, know what that requires of you and, most important of all, ask for it. You cannot rely on others working it out for you. You need to gain competitive advantage – which is the central purpose of this book.

How to get promoted

There are five universal criteria that determine, in most organisations, who will get promoted and who won't. Though the importance of each will vary by circumstance, these are nearly always considerations (whether acknowledged or not) that you should pay attention to.

1. Exceptional performance in your current role

This is far and away the most important. It is unlikely you will get promoted if you are not considered to be among the strongest performers at your current level.

2. Leadership potential

Promotion nearly always means you will have greater responsibility over other people. This could be more people in total and/or more senior and experienced people. As previously noted, you are likely to find yourself in leadership positions from very early in your career, and your ability to develop and lead brilliant teams is a skill that will supercharge your progress. A very common reason given for not promoting competent people is the perception that they are not good leaders – so make sure that isn't you. The more senior you become, the more your ability to run effective teams will become the most significant factor in determining your rate of progress and future potential.

3. Growth driver (or, I'm putting a man on the moon)

Those who add meaningful value to the projects that the organisation values the most highly will be most highly valued in turn.

For the majority of organisations, growth is the priority objective. There are those for whom this isn't the case, in the public sector, for example, but every well-run organisation will have a single overriding objective that they expect their key people to be focused on.

In 1962, President John F. Kennedy visited NASA for the first time. During his tour of the facility, he met a janitor carrying a broom down the hallway. The President asked the man what he did, and the janitor gave him what became a famous reply, 'Mr President, I'm helping put a man on the moon.'

If you want to progress quickly, you need to understand what the priority objective is and work out how you are contributing towards it.

4. Alignment with culture

'Fit' matters when people get hired and it matters when they get promoted. All organisations want people who embody the company's values and culture, who they trust, like, want to work with and that others want to work for. Being this person gets you promoted more quickly.

5. Visibility

In order to get promoted, it is not enough to do a good job; you also need to be seen to be doing a good job. The key decision-makers need to know you and have first-hand experience of you as a person, not just your work.

You should make sure your successes and contributions are known and that you have a wide network of connections across the organisation as well as strong relationships with your colleagues, your boss and their peers.

At each step in our careers, before focusing on what comes next, we should endeavour to establish what is required to be excellent in the job we have today. Do not become so obsessed with the next job that you give too little time or attention to your current one; that will only lead you to a vicious circle of underperformance and frustration.

Understanding excellence today

I recently saw a post on LinkedIn which claimed to show evidence of how standards at work have fallen. It was a job description for Saatchi & Saatchi, the advertising agency, from the 1980s. It listed 209 tasks the candidate should excel at in order to succeed.

How to survive as a Saatchi & Saatchi suit.

Being an outstanding "suit" is no easy task. Being an outstanding "Saatchis" suit is even more difficult.

Saatchi & Saatchi has high standards and high expectations of each and every member of the team. But we are only human. Sometimes we make mistakes. Other times we don't know what is expected, and other times we won't know the best way of achieving our objectives.

This poster is a collection of pointers, 'tips' if you like, to help you achieve success in your endeavours. They reflect both the 'Saatchi' attitude and practical ways of doing your job better.

If you use the poster correctly, it should help you make the right decision in those circumstances where a little help really would be helpful.

Go for it, and good luck!

1. Nothing is impossible.

2. Advertising is a collective process. Use 'we' and avoid 'I'. 'We' is both truthful and reassuring.

3. Saatchi & Saatchi is the best agency in Singapore. Always behave in a way that adds to its reputation.

4. Remember good manners. Treat everyone with respect.

5. Think Big – big ideas lead to big results.

6. Admit your mistakes, learn from them, move on.

7. A big task is rarely accomplished with a little ad.

8. You're in the driver's seat – drive your business into the future.

9. Never be afraid to ask… an inquiring mind is an asset.

10. Search for solutions, not problems.

11. Treat the Agency as if it were your own.

12. Treat every advertisement as your own. Mentally substitute your name where the logo is. Still proud of it.

13. Remember, technology lets you do many things – use satellites, hire phones, [. . .]

An adaption of a section of the original advertisement.

Two hundred and nine!

The person who unearthed this dubious gem claimed that more of this type of thinking was what we needed at work today.

Errr.

Can you imagine starting a job and being given a list of over 200 things you need to excel at? Nobody is excellent at 200 things. Most of us would settle for excellence at just one thing. Where would we begin? How could we focus? How would we decide how to spend our time to greatest effect?

If we want to get promoted, we must ensure that we know what being brilliant at our current role means in practice. It sounds obvious, but many people, even very senior people, do not. So many drift through work on autopilot, assuming what is required of them without ever thinking to explicitly check.

You should start with your job description. In my experience, job descriptions (like contracts) are mostly used only as a last resort when something goes wrong. This isn't very helpful. If there isn't one, ask for it. If you have to, compose one yourself and discuss it with your boss.

However, a job description, though important, is not typically enough. What is most important is understanding what your boss wants and needs from you beyond the formal language. This is what will most determine your immediate rate of progress. We are employed by a company but we work for our bosses. They are the most important person in our working lives. Our job is to help them succeed at theirs, and vice versa. They too have their own career ambitions; what they need are people who are going to help them get there. This is how to become indispensable.

You should ask your boss this question at least once a year:

What is the most important thing I need
to do in order to succeed at my job?

An interesting variation on this is:

> What do I need to do in order to help
> you [your boss] succeed at yours?

These questions lead to obvious follow-ups, such as:

> I'd like your help to enable me to do [. . .] more effectively.

> I'd like more opportunity to [. . .].

> I'd like to do more of that, but [. . .] makes it difficult for me. Can you help me overcome that barrier?

Bosses sometimes dislike conversations about promotions, but they mostly understand success. They implicitly understand that somebody who is succeeding in their role is beneficial to them and makes their life easier. Similarly, they understand that somebody who is failing holds them back and makes their life more difficult.

A discussion with your boss about personal success is often more useful than one only about promotion. Promotion is all about you, whereas success is about you *and* them. This is a very practical way to gain an understanding of what is really required of you.

Over the years, I have found that the best way to have such conversations is informally – over a coffee, perhaps. It signals ambition, but in a way that places you at the heart of a team. It is especially useful with a new boss as they may have different opinions to the one you had before. As always, write down what is agreed and email it to them; it makes a useful starting point for your next conversation.

Understanding what next

Once you are clear what success looks like in the job you are currently doing and you feel you are well on the way to mastering it, you should begin to understand what is required of you to achieve the next step up. You might ask your boss:

I am ambitious and would like [job goes here].
What do I have to do in order to be considered
for this [role/promotion/opportunity]?

The combination of this question and those in the preceding section enables you to have a productive conversation about success today and about your future progress – all done in a responsible and professional manner. Your boss may tell you now is not the time to talk about new roles or promotions, but even that is useful (if maybe unwelcome) feedback. You shouldn't see such a response as final or as the end of the conversation. A useful and respectful follow-up question might be:

Can you help me understand why, so I can ensure
that I am focusing my energy in the right areas?

If they flag areas where personal development is required, ask for their help and support. Even better, make their life easier by suggesting the type of support you would like. Conclude by thanking them, even if you haven't liked what you heard, and asking:

When would it be appropriate for us to discuss this again?

As always, write down whatever is agreed, email it to them and any other relevant stakeholders – your HR rep, for example – and use those notes as the basis for the discussion next time you meet. It is always a good idea to form a productive relationship with your colleagues in HR; they are rarely decision-makers, but are often important influencers when it comes to key career decisions, so get them on your side.

(However, do not allow your boss to push you to HR for all the answers. You work for your boss, not for HR – and they're the one who has the greatest influence on your experiences at work, how you learn and how you progress.)

Sometimes, your boss might find it difficult to immediately answer the questions above. If so, don't judge them. They're not always easy questions to answer. Even if they can't give you a crisp answer right away, the questions are still powerful ways to start a great conversation. As always: if you don't ask, you're likely to be left guessing – and I know from personal experience how very easy it is to guess wrong.

Ambitious vs being a pain in the arse

Written in a single condensed block of copy, the above advice could be interpreted as being rather pushy, or worse, making you appear a downright pain in the arse. Not ideal, especially around your boss.

Sometimes you will not like the response you get from them. Sometimes you will have to be patient, and other times you will experience frustrating setbacks. Sometimes things just don't work out. This is frustrating, but you cannot simply revert to asking the same questions again and again, hoping for different answers.

Only by asking clear questions will you have a chance of getting clear answers. But, as with all communication, it is as important to listen as it is to ask. Simply being demanding and filtering out the responses you don't like will not help you, indeed will be counter-productive. The point of getting clarity is not to get answers that you like, it is to get answers that are honest and useful.

People who don't listen are a pain in the arse. So, if you ask, you need to make sure you listen and then act. If you don't, you may end up in a worse position than when you began.

Always have answers to your own questions

Asking smart questions is a good thing in both work and life (although asking smart-arse questions designed to catch people out is definitely not). However, questions, even clever ones, are a lot easier to ask than answers are to find. We should therefore endeavour to never ask a question to which we have not formulated a proposed solution. This is a really important lesson to learn.

One of the most indispensable habits is to develop a problem-solving mindset. That is not the same as having all the answers, we never will. Rather, it is understanding that our role is to try to find solutions (as opposed to problems) and to help others do the same. We should therefore never take a question to our boss without having potential answers in mind. It is the attitude of being solution-focused that matters far more than whether they agree. It also makes it easier for them to begin to think through their options and potential solutions.

A reasonable response when asked an important or difficult question, especially by somebody who works for you is:

What do you recommend?

Or

What do you suggest/think?

When you sit down with your boss, who that morning had a row with their partner and in two hours has a stressful meeting scheduled with their own boss, it is reasonable for them to first ask for your suggestions. It's what I would do.

You don't have to be right. You simply have to demonstrate that you've given it some intelligent thought. Your objective is a productive, mutually beneficial outcome, not to add to your boss's workload.

This is also a good behaviour to adopt with those who work *for* you. If asked by a subordinate for help or advice, always start by asking for their recommended solution. Your job is not to be problem-solver in chief, however good that makes you feel. It is to help your team get better at solving problems themselves. This is what Pink's *autonomy* means in practice (Chapter 4).

Indispensable people are always focused on finding solutions, not problems. Problems are ten a penny; solutions are worth their weight in gold.

A note on industry standards

You cannot progress in any career without first ensuring that you have the necessary skills and/or qualifications. Much of the learning we do at work is informal or on the job, and I wrote this book because I believe much of that is done badly. However, sometimes progress requires you to undertake formal training or to achieve professional qualifications. If these are relevant to your situation, you must make sure you are clear on what they are and how you are going to get them.

A good employer will provide a road map outlining your access to the necessary training, whether for success in your current role or your next. If they don't, you must ask for one, to ensure you understand what the training requirements for career progress are and when you will be able to undertake them. Note that in all conversations such as this, your bosses are inevitably going to say no from time to time. When that happens, ask what the barriers to access for you are and what you need to do to overcome them.

If your company has an HR department or a Learning and Development (L&D) department, they may be responsible for formal training. If you aren't able to get a clear answer from your boss you should ask them. As always, be respectful and listen properly to the answers. Being keen is always a good thing; being demanding is not.

In many organisations, training and development is rationed. Spaces are limited because of cost, but also to drive a sense of value through scarcity; people win their place through recommendation and/or merit. You should endeavour to get on these programmes. They are a measure of progress, valuable opportunities to learn, of a higher standard than more widely accessible programmes, and are great for networking and for your CV.

In some companies the selection criteria can be opaque. In a competitive landscape, you cannot rely on others stepping aside to give you the last spot. You shouldn't be unreasonable or unrealistic, but you should make it clear you would like a place, that you would make the most of the opportunity, and demonstrate why you deserve it. If it's a 'no' the first time, then make sure you understand why and what more you need to do to be considered next time round.

Even if a particular programme is intended for people with several years more experience than you, there is nothing to be lost, and much to be gained, by politely making it clear that one day you would like to attend and by asking to understand what it is you'll have to do in order to win a place in due course.

At work, the squeaky wheel gets the oil. So (politely) squeak away.

Pay rises

If I had a pound for every time an HR director had told me that pay is far from the top of most people's requirements to be happy in their jobs, I'd be a rich man indeed. I simply don't buy it (excuse the pun). I accept that it's not the only factor, but pay really matters, and a key measure of progress is the rate at which we get pay rises. They are also one of the most emotive and difficult topics to confront in the workplace.

It is unusual for people to get a pay rise when they don't expect it. Every rise I have ever received I had to ask for. And I usually got less than I wanted. On one occasion, after a particularly underwhelming rise, my boss snapped back at me, 'What the bloody hell do you want, a cherry on it?'

For many people, asking for a raise is uncomfortable. Yet it is an essential ingredient for a successful career. It's a balance. Asking for the right amount at the right time is good (if sometimes unwelcome). Asking for too much – either for something you patently don't deserve or asking too frequently – is not.

If you understand what your boss needs from you, and you understand the organisation's requirements for your current role and for the next one, then you can form a realistic view on whether now is the time to ask for a rise, a bigger bonus, more training or more responsibility. If you find yourself in a position where you think you deserve a promotion while your boss thinks you're not meeting their standards, then there is something amiss that you need to get to the bottom of.

These days, it's relatively easy to find information on pay scales – both within your company and across the industry as a whole. Some companies are more formal about pay rates than others but, whatever they may tell you, there is always discretion in what people are paid and there is always a spectrum of salaries available for any given role. This means that some people are at the top and some at the bottom. You are unlikely to get a figure above that upper limit (though the discretion point stands), but if you feel you've done a great job of what has been asked, then you can reasonably request an above-average salary for the role, as well as a discussion about what you need to do to move up to the next level.

Asking for a raise

It's sometimes difficult to say what we really think. Or to ask for what we really want. You might hope that, by being somewhat oblique, your boss will guess what it is you really want, or figure it out for themselves, but this is unlikely to work. When we're busy, we are all tempted to take the path of least resistance – and that's certainly true for your boss. If you don't ask clearly for what you want, they are unlikely to spontaneously add you to their to-do list, especially when it comes to a sensitive subject such as pay.

The first step is to be honest with yourself, which is not always as easy as it sounds. What do you really want and can your boss or your current employer deliver that? If the issue at its core is that you hate your job and you would actually like to go and open a herb farm, then they aren't going to be able to help you. If you've been offered another job for more money, but would rather stay, they won't know unless you are explicit about it.

It's amazing how often people choose to leave a job they enjoy because they find this easier than asking for a raise. To be clear – that's not because they didn't get the raise, but because they felt too awkward to even ask for it. Many regret this eventually. It's a bad way to manage a career and it happens all the time.

Here's what you need to know and do to give yourself the best chance of getting the raise you deserve. And, if you don't get what you want, to make sure you do the next time round.

1. The context

Salaries are one of an organisation's biggest costs, so every company tries hard to keep them as low as they can, even those that pretend they don't. Company-wide, they will have a provision every year for the total amount allocated for raises (as a rule of thumb in established businesses, this will usually be expressed as a percentage roughly in line with inflation). It is almost certain that you will be asking for more than this, which is why it's so competitive; the more you get, the less there is for others. Therefore, the case you're making is not simply why you deserve more, but implicitly why you deserve more than somebody else – though you should not frame it in those terms.

2. Preparation

The secret sauce in so many situations at work is preparation, and it is key when asking for a raise. You need to be clear with yourself about how much you're going to ask for, why you're asking for it now and why you deserve it. Three good reasons are enough; adding more means ending up with a forgettable list on which your big points are obscured by minutiae.

Once you're clear on what you want, write it down as notes, especially if you feel uncomfortable expressing it. If necessary, take those notes into the meeting with you. It will help. Your boss would prefer to know what you're thinking, even if they might not like what they hear.

If you can convince yourself that you are delivering against the targets your boss has set you, then you have a reasonable chance of convincing them of your case.

3. JFDI

Annual reviews, though often inefficient, are an important time for you to formally set out your ambitions and expectations. Some companies try to limit when raises are given to a specific point in the financial year, but that doesn't mean you can only ask during those times. If you're proactively seeking a raise or a promotion, you should avoid exceptionally busy times such as the financial year-end, important sales periods or holidays.

That all said, there is no time like the present. Do not put this conversation off indefinitely. As I outlined in Chapter 6, when it comes to difficult conversations, don't overthink it, Just F**king Do It.

4. What your boss is thinking

The single most important thing for you to understand before asking for a raise is that it's almost never your boss's money, and is therefore a way bigger deal for you than them. Because at the end of the day – it is your money.

However, because it's not their money, it also means that it's often not wholly within their power to say yes – whether they admit that or not. Throughout your career, you'll discover that a lot more people have the authority to say no than the authority to say yes.

Therefore, the response you are most likely to get at first will be non-committal. This is fine. Your boss will want to buy themselves time to think and get approval if they agree with you. Thus, your preparation matters not just for the conversation with them, but also to ensure they are able to make your case to others.

Negotiation

Some larger employers have a structured process for how and when pay rises are given. There are good reasons for this. If they have many employees, they don't want to find themselves in a continual process of pay discussions with thousands of people. Most also have formal (or informal) pay bands which dictate what they pay for a given role.

This means that your employer may wish to control the timing and the terms of discussions around your pay and career. They have their reasons, but it is important you continue to follow the principles outlined here. They may have their process, but you must have your plan. They aren't going to throw their rules out of the window just for you, but nor should you be a passive actor. You need to put yourself, not their process, first – and, as discussed already, have clarity over your own desires and ambitions.

When discussing career progress and/or money with your employer, it's important to recognise these conversations for what they are: namely, a renegotiation of your terms of employment. The company buys your time, so at what rate would you now like to sell it? This can be a better salary, but also additional investment in you – for example, in the form of professional development or different working patterns. Remember, neither party is doing the other a favour. You are all employees. They need you, or you wouldn't be there, and they have a value that they put on your time. It's not wrong or inappropriate for you to ask for more money, nor is it wrong for them to interrogate your request before reaching a conclusion. It is for this reason that you should be prepared for such negotiations to extend over several meetings as you explore each other's positions.

The first steps in any effective negotiation are those we have already covered: preparation, clarity of objective and honesty (with yourself at least). Having a positive and mutually respectful relationship with your boss will also make it more likely that you will both get a good outcome. If you have a bad relationship, it will make it much harder.

As with any negotiation, you must ensure you understand clearly what has been proposed to you. For example, you may win the promotion and pay rise, but the company might expect you to work different hours or less flexibly. You should understand their reasons. What do you need to do, by when, and what support will they offer you along the way? What are the milestones you both need to hit? You must then decide whether you think this is a reasonable proposal – and what to do if not.

BATNA: The best alternative to a negotiated agreement

What happens if you do everything right, do your homework, prepare well, have a mutually respectful relationship with your boss, make your case . . . and you still don't get to a reasonable outcome. What do you do then?

Professional negotiators always start with a BATNA (Best Alternative To a Negotiated Agreement). In other words: a plan for what to do if the negotiation fails. Another expression people use is 'a red line' – a point they will not go beyond. For example, we may see a house we love and make a deliberately low offer to try to explore the other party's red line. The problem in this example is that somebody else may get there more quickly if you misjudge your start-point. Or the seller may conclude that you're not serious.

In some ways, negotiations at work are more straightforward. Unlike a house purchase, where there are often multiple parties involved, here there are only two: you and your employer.

If you don't get what you want, you must first try to find common ground and perhaps a path towards how and when you might get there. A simple 'no' is a bad outcome for everyone. It's a bad outcome for them because it means you walk away dissatisfied and potentially angry, but it is you who it most affects.

Companies often hide behind bureaucracy and process as reasons to say no. For example, they may set a maximum possible percentage for rises, or require a certain amount of experience before a promotion or eligibility for a particular training programme. However, though companies try hard to protect these principles, they are nearly always flexible. They are used as an excuse to not give you what you want by making it appear as though negotiation is impossible. You must decide whether you believe them. You always have options; you just have to decide whether you have any that are better than where you are at already.

Take your time if you need it. Sometimes it's easy to just say yes, and it's tempting for your employer to gently bully you into doing so. But an outcome that you're not happy with suits neither party. Professional negotiators consider success to be an outcome that leaves both parties feeling like they have got the best of the deal.

When you are negotiating with an employer, remember that it's only personal for one party involved – you. It is not personal for them, no matter what they say. It is not their time, money, career or mortgage that is being discussed, it is yours. If the negotiation goes badly, it's not something that will keep them awake at night fuming. But that may well be the case for you.

At work, your BATNA is what your options might be if you do not get what you want from the negotiation. Understanding these helps you evaluate the offer that has been made to you, not just against what you asked for, but against your alternatives. Furthermore, it ensures that you have a plan that is based around your own ambitions rather than purely around the expectations and limitations of your employer. A good BATNA helps you maintain a sense of control over where it is you would like to get to.

Finding other ways

If you ultimately don't get what you want, then you need to consider whether you simply shrug and put up with it or leave to spend your time elsewhere. Sometimes the latter is the right thing to do – you should not simply suck it up. However, changing jobs brings with it a whole bunch of new unknowns, so it's not an option that should be taken in haste or anger. Before you resort to leaving, there are a number of avenues you can explore to try to see if you can get back on track:

- Timelines: Ask, if not now, when? What would have to change for their position to move closer to yours?
- Learning: If they feel you lack requisite skills, how can they help you gain them? As always, ensure you come to this conversation with ideas of your own.
- Internal transfer: In some large companies, it might be possible to transfer department, or even country, in order to gain a different kind of learning and experience. Don't be afraid to ask. It's okay for you to be disappointed with the outcome of the negotiation, and it is illustrative of your professionalism and commitment that you are prepared to explore alternative solutions.
- Professional mentor or coach: Can they help you find a coach or mentor to develop both your soft and hard skills? This could be part of an existing internal mentoring programme or them funding an external coach.

- Internal development programmes: Are there programmes within the company you would like to be considered for? How can you get on to them?

- External development programmes: Are there programmes you have found outside the company that you believe would help you close any skill gaps? Can your employer fund or part-fund them? Many companies have schemes that allow them to do just that.

- Third party support: Ask a third party (perhaps somebody senior to you, but not your immediate boss) to spend a couple of hours and workshop with you how you might close the gap between your expectations of your next step and your boss's. Draw on their experience of what it takes to progress in the company. This person may also give you a sense check – perhaps you're doing great, but being a little unreasonable or unrealistic? HR departments can be very good at providing this kind of support (or suggesting somebody who can).

The point is: have a plan. You will not always get what you want. But even in that unhappy circumstance, there are often ways you can get back on track and close the gap between what you want, and what your employer believes is appropriate.

This can be difficult. You may be angry, upset, feel hurt or that your efforts have been ignored or dismissed. You may see others who you believe to be less deserving progress while you do not. This happens to everybody at some point. These situations are not final, nor need they be fatal for your prospects. If you respond well and are willing to learn and listen to feedback, you can still make progress. Employers are impressed with people who are prepared and able to do this. After all – they might be right.

Many years ago, I was passed over three times in six years for the same promotion. Each time, a new hire took the role instead. I was furious and disappointed. I found it unjust and unfair. However, I look back now and think: they were right, I was wrong – I just wasn't ready. And I got there in the end.

You're the boss of you

Managing your career requires you to be proactive and clear. Even if you work for somebody who is good for your career, you must know what you want so that they are best able to help you. And if you are going to learn and progress you must be prepared to hear the bad as well as the good.

If you have a grand overarching vision for your career, great. But if you don't, just ask yourself these uncomplicated questions, which will help ensure you continue to progress year by year.

- *What change(s) would enable me to enjoy my job more or find it more rewarding?*
- *What jobs are there in this company that I would love to do – how do I build a path towards them?*
- *What new (career-related) skills would I like to learn/ develop over the next twelve months?*
- *What (career-related) experience would I like to gain over the next twelve months?*
- *What are the aspects of my job that I dislike the most – how can I change this over the next twelve months?*

These are not grand 'career-planning' questions, but they are good questions to regularly ask yourself – especially before conversations with your boss, whether initiated by them or by you. Once you've begun, I'm sure you will be able to think of others that are even more specific to your own situation.

To progress in your career, you must be organised in how you ask for what you want, and listen carefully to the answers. Expect it to be a negotiation. Things will not always go your way and progress will be more rapid in some years than in others. However, if you approach the conversations with your own ideas, with energy and goodwill, you will ultimately get to where you want to go.

The best any of us can ever hope for is intelligent, but imperfect, progress.

CHAPTER 9

Networking: A Bluffer's Guide

Many years ago, when I was still an undergraduate, I was staying with a friend whose ambitious older sister was home for the weekend. Over dinner, she moaned at length about a conference she was due to attend the following week. If it was going to be so awful, why on earth are you going, her mum asked. 'Well, because it will be a great networking opportunity,' she replied. (The dinner was incidentally memorable to me for another reason: I got told off by my friend's mum for cutting up a baguette incorrectly. But I'll save that for the next book. And my therapist.)

My friend's sister's reply flummoxed me. I was an admittedly sheltered twenty-year-old, midway through a degree in engineering, and the only networks I could think of were related to heavy-current electrical circuits – and I knew it wasn't that, she wasn't the engineering type. After overcoming my baguette shame, I eventually summoned up the courage to ask. Since that first explanation to the present day, the words 'networking event' have always made me shudder.

I am not a natural networker. I never grew to love it as some do, but throughout my career I grew to understand and value the power of professional networks, and consequently found ways to overcome my fears and hesitancy – ultimately becoming passably proficient.

Here, then, is the hesitant networker's bluffer's guide.

Why professional networks matter

Professional networks are accelerants to the careers of those who have and nurture them, and potential barriers to entry for those who do not. I meet many people, particularly those starting out in their careers, who feel intimidated by their lack of connections. However, networks can be built and nurtured, even by those who are not naturals (like me).

Like everything else, networking is something that can be improved through practice and familiarity. It requires determination, clarity of purpose, a willingness to get out of your comfort zone (a bit), practice and perhaps a little courage. But no great talent. Over time, anybody can get better at it, build connections and friendships that can last a lifetime, and add depth and enjoyment to their career. Social media has made it easier than ever to find like-minded people or groups and maintain relationships with them – many who you may never meet in person. The key to success is to see networking as a route to building meaningful relationships rather than simply a transactional process.

How professional networks help your career

Professional networks are not solely about the exchange of business cards or building up our social media profiles. They can help our careers in five broad ways, all of which will be very useful at different times:

1. Visibility

You may find this annoying. I know I have from time to time, but career success isn't simply about doing a great job. You have to be seen to be doing a great job. Visibility matters a great deal in our careers, both inside and outside our organisation. It's not enough for people to see you in a meeting (for example); they have to know you, which means speaking up and building relationships with them. Be respectful, actively listen and always be polite to others, because you just never know when you're going to come across them again – and maybe even need their support. Internal networking (getting to know and be known by your colleagues and bosses) is an often overlooked but important part of networking.

2. Finding new opportunities

These could be inside or outside the organisation where you currently work. Having good visibility and a strong network improves your chances of promotion, allows you to find great new opportunities externally, and improves your chances of getting hired.

As we've established, the recruitment process is a notoriously unreliable means to understanding either a prospective employer or employee, and a strong network helps both parties get what they want. Even in the most rigorous recruitment processes, pre-existing personal connections or introductions help both parties.

3. Finding new talent

At a certain point in your career, being able to find great people to work in your team becomes a critical task. It's not easy. The better people are, the more choices they have. Why should they choose you? Having a strong network affords you access to a pool of people who are already at least partly known to you – and you to them. A network can also serve as a means of connecting you to people who can help you in your search. Both of these factors improve your ability to attract more than your fair share of the best people into your team(s), which is a critical skill for successful leaders.

4. Mentoring

At certain times, we all benefit from mentorship, and a strong network is a great place to start. Many people find becoming a mentor very rewarding. Your network is a great way for you to give back and help those who you think could learn from your experiences and mistakes, as well as to find someone who can do the same for you.

5. Knowledge and information sharing

A strong professional network allows you to stay connected to trends, ideas and the latest best practice, ensuring you stay on top of what's happening right across your industry – and beyond.

Overcoming network-a-phobia

Beth Comstock, former vice chair of General Electric and author of *Imagine It Forward*, once told me that she had determined, early on in her career, that being an introvert wasn't going to stop her from building a great network. She approached it as an arachnophobe might overcome their fear of spiders, starting small and moving gradually up to the full tarantula.

There is no great secret to networking: simply preparation, practice and perhaps, as with arachnophobia, a little courage. These will be the most important determinants of your progress. This advice could be the subheading for this book. It's how you get better at everything. There is, after all, only one way to become a great musician, and that is by getting started as a bad one.

Self-limiting beliefs

What most holds us back in life is ourselves – it is first and foremost us we have to shove out of the way if we want to fulfil our ambitions. We tell ourselves that those confident people we see have something we do not. Yet the people who love networking don't have a special elixir that they take before walking into the room. They're just people, like you and me, who each have their own unique blend of strengths, weaknesses and insecurities. We have no way of knowing if they are naturals at it or if they too once felt as we do; whether they too are a mass of boiling emotions inside. We can't be somebody else, but we can make sure we get out of our own way.

The biggest barriers we face as we contemplate walking into that room full of people are those that live in our own minds: not what everybody else is thinking, but the stories we are telling ourselves. Overcoming this is perhaps the greatest barrier for many of us, but it can be done – and it's worth the effort to do so.

1. Be kind to yourself

Your ambition today is not to miraculously develop the networking genius of Barack Obama; it is more modest and achievable than that. You may in time grow to love the exhilaration of meeting and building relationships with strangers, but that's not your ambition today. Today's about getting started.

Ask yourself what it is that holds you back. Be specific – not simply that walking into a room of strangers is intimidating, but why? What is it that you fear? What makes you uncomfortable. Is it rejection, not knowing what to say, making yourself look silly, that you feel like you don't belong in that room?

For me, it was always the latter. I don't know why – it doesn't really matter why. Even when I held very senior roles, I still felt it. These are not rational, carefully argued statements of fact; they are emotion, stories I was telling myself. Stories others found ridiculous. Understand them as that, and they begin to feel smaller.

As you stand at the doorway looking in, remind yourself that there are many others in that room who feel the same as you. You are not alone. No matter how intimidating it seems, keep in mind that there are more people in the room who feel like you than those who don't – and all of them are just looking for somebody nice to talk to to get them through it. Don't set yourself unrealistic goals. Don't try to run before you can walk. And most importantly, don't beat yourself up if sometimes you just can't face it.

It would be disingenuous of me to suggest that you're going to click with everybody you meet. We know that isn't true. It can be tempting to ruminate on encounters that were awkward or went nowhere, but it's important you accept these as simply occasionally inevitable. They are not a reflection of who you are – they are just a boring and forgettable conversation. Nothing more.

Instead, celebrate the conversations and introductions you had that you enjoyed, or that were useful, or where there was an easy route to a follow-up. As every general knows, you should reinforce success, never defeat. Those that didn't work out, sobeit. Imagine them as pages you release into the wind and move on.

I once attended a grand black-tie event (a ridiculous dress code which incidentally makes already intimidating forums even more exclusionary, pretentious and stuffy – they should get in the sea) and, summoning my courage, introduced myself to a very senior figure in the industry. We had a passable if stilted conversation for a couple of minutes until, hearing a voice he recognised behind him, he swivelled on his heel mid-sentence and struck up a whole new conversation with the newcomer. He didn't bother to introduce me and I was left studying the back of his head for a few moments before shuffling away on my own. It was so bad it was funny, and ultimately useful as it gave me something to talk to other people about for the rest of the evening. Most people are not like this.

And if you come across those that are, just make sure to mention them when you write your book.

2. Start small (or progressive exposure theory)

You might find that once you get started at networking, you're a natural. It's not as unlikely as it sounds. If you don't, then take an incremental approach. Beth Comstock told me that she explicitly set herself targets. At first, at each event she attended, she would introduce herself to just one other person. As she became more confident, she began introducing herself to two people per event, then three, and so on. Soon, she stopped counting. It gets easier, but only if you get started. Before you know it, you'll have a wide and eclectic network of contacts – and some new friends. Everything is difficult until it becomes easy.

There is a virtuous circle to networking. At first, you may look at the bustling room and see only strangers. In time, however, simply by regularly showing up, you will begin to see the same people again and again. Soon, those people will acquire names and job titles and backgrounds. Occasionally you'll spot the person who turned their back on you mid-conversation and can redeploy your anecdote about the event. The room stops being a sea of strangers, instead becoming one dotted with familiar faces. And the more people you know, the more likely it is they will introduce you to those you don't.

3. Find a wing (wo)man

Most people find walking into large rooms of strangers intimidating. Therefore, an obvious solution is to find somebody to go with. The easiest place to start is with a colleague or friend. If they feel the same as you, then they'll be thankful for the support. And if they are more confident, then all the better; you can learn from them and bob along in their slipstream.

Though less intimidating than going solo, a downside of this approach is that you can unwittingly find yourself tethered to the person you arrived with, and meet nobody else. Between you, you have to determine to meet others, even if you do it together – and hold each other accountable.

Also, be explicit with your co-pilot. The reason you're going is to grow your network and to do that you need a plan (like this one). Discuss it with them. They may be grateful for the help.

4. Fish where the fish are

It might be that you have lots of opportunities to meet people, but shy away from them. Or it might be that you don't know where to begin. Where does all this 'networking' even happen?

An easy and useful place to start is where you work. Use the company's existing forums to meet others. These could be through formal company meetings and events, or through planned social events. Are there people in your organisation who seem particularly well connected? Are there opportunities to learn from them? People like being asked for advice and, if you are respectful of them and their time, most will be happy to help. Just connecting with them in an informal way is a great start. Don't overthink it.

All industries also have trade bodies which host regular events that are generally either free or cost very little to attend. These usually vary from the intimate to the very large and are a great place to meet like-minded people in your industry – not least because everybody is there for the same reason as you. And because you're in the same industry, you have ready-made common ground.

Many industries also have thriving ancillary businesses around them, such as recruitment or consulting agencies. These businesses hold networking events from time to time as they are keen to drum up work, connections, influence and, yes, build their network. You should look for such opportunities to build your network beyond your employer, and these are a relatively easy and productive place to start.

Platforms like LinkedIn also have many forums and groups that are both industry- and interest group-specific which offer a mix of virtual and in-person meet-ups. Once you begin to look, you'll find lots of places which will welcome you with open arms.

Of course, you will find some events more interesting and more useful than others. But as you get into the rhythm of it, you'll get better at finding the events that most suit you. You will also quickly get to the point where you're getting more invites than you can or want to accept.

5. Frequency matters

Networking is not a difficult skill to learn, but you cannot learn it, nor overcome your anxieties, if you never practise. If opportunities do not organically arise very often, then you have to hunt them out. If you only go to one event a year it will take an impossibly long time to overcome your anxieties and to grow your network. You don't need to become obsessive, but, if you're serious about making progress, you cannot allow months to slide by.

6. What on earth shall I say . . . ?

Have you noticed how some people just seem to know what to say in any situation? If this isn't you, it can be a major barrier when meeting people for the first time. However, as always, preparation can make all the difference.

If possible, before you go to an event (even a small one – perhaps especially a small one), do a little research on who is likely to be there. Nowadays, LinkedIn makes this easier than ever. If there are specific people you'd like to connect with, then take the time in advance to find out a little about them, maybe even drop them a note to say you're looking forward to meeting. Good networkers always do this. It's not weird, or stalking. It's how networking works and is one of the reasons LinkedIn exists.

Always remember, just because you don't see somebody prepare, it doesn't mean they didn't do it. Many of those people who make it look easy are just great at preparing and diligent about practice.

You can also prepare questions in advance. Once you've broken the ice, it gets a lot easier. Some useful introductory questions are:

What do you think about the [theme] of this event?

What brings you to this event?

Is there something specific you
are hoping to learn at this event?

Who are you most looking forward to hearing speak?

What advice would you give somebody
just starting out in this industry/field?

What did you think of the last speaker?

I'm enjoying this so far; are there other events
you've been to that you found useful?

I saw your presentation/article about [. . .]
I'd love to hear more about it.

I'd love to pick your brains on [. . .]

I see we have a common connection.
How do you know them?

And don't forget to tell them your name and where you work (or an equivalent piece of introductory and relevant information).

The above are very general questions that just about anybody can find a way to answer. Have a couple up your sleeve before you arrive; try some different ones out. You don't need lots – you can use the same ones with everybody you meet. It'll soon become second nature.

People also like being complimented or asked their opinion – especially senior people. If you know who they are, perhaps mention a piece of work, a speech or an article they have written. Ask them for advice. It doesn't really matter how you begin, just get going.

Overthinking and perfectionism can make us freeze. We fear making ourselves look silly or drying up, or people not wanting to talk to us. However, remember that the major purpose of networking events is for people to meet each other, so the people who are there actively want to meet you.

7. Be an active listener

A great way to get a conversation started – and to keep it going – is to ask questions. People like talking about themselves; it's a subject we are all experts in. We also like to believe that others are interested in us. A successful introductory conversation is one where we gradually discover information about each other by asking questions and, more importantly, by listening to each other's answers.

Active listening at networking events is very important. The example of the man who turned his back on me is an extreme one. Most people are not so rude. But the person who permanently scans the room over your shoulder is more common. Do not be this person. Your objective is not just to superficially interact, it is to build a relationship. That's not going to happen if people think you're rude, arrogant or uninterested.

Listening properly to what people say allows us to ask sensible follow-up questions. A series of disconnected questions is rather disconcerting and suggests that the person we're talking to isn't listening to us.

Similarly, people who just talk about themselves are boring. Try to redirect your focus from what you're going to say, to what you can learn. Learning requires enthusiasm, lots of questions and active listening, all three of which make you a great person to talk to. After all, you don't just want to meet people, you want them to introduce you to others – and they're far more likely to do so if they like you.

8. Manage your online profile

Social media, LinkedIn in particular, has become a powerful professional networking tool. People routinely look at the attendance lists for events and check them out on social media beforehand. You should too. Use it to connect in advance with people you'd like to meet as well as a means of following up with those you met.

You should ensure your online presence looks professional and is up-to-date. If you have the inclination and energy, occasional blogs or posts make your page feel more energetic and alive. You might, for example, write short opinion pieces on the events you have attended. However, this is not for everybody and is not essential. What matters is that your page looks as you would wish to be perceived. LinkedIn is often the first introduction strangers will have to you in a professional context. A new boss is likely to check out their team online. Customers and colleagues all use it to understand a little about who you are, just as you do them.

Almost nobody gets hired these days without the employer and recruiter visiting their LinkedIn page. It can be surprisingly powerful in framing expectations; first impressions really do count. Ensure you have an appropriate photograph – if in doubt, play it safe – and that all of the relevant sections have been completed, including education, interests and employment history. These days, people are far more aware of the opportunities and pitfalls of social media, but horror stories still pop up. Whether you like it or not, some employers will check your social media profile – not just LinkedIn, but Instagram, TikTok, Twitter (X), Snap and so on. Don't be naïve. I'll leave the rest to your discretion and imagination.

Finding your own way

Having a varied and rich professional network can be rewarding, enjoyable and very useful for our careers, but they don't just happen – we get back what we put in. Because we're all different, some of us are better at developing and nurturing networks than others. The objective here is not to encourage you to become somebody you're not; it's to help you become the best version of who you already are. It is not to be a frantic accumulator of LinkedIn followers; it is to find a way that works for you and to reassure you that it is not as difficult or as intimidating as it might at first seem.

For some people, networking can feel inauthentic and forced, but in reality it's simply a way to meet more people, most of whom are just like you. We all have friends and networks in other parts of our life, so we can all do it, and when it comes to our careers, the effort is worthwhile.

The good news is that there are many ways to build your network beyond standing next to the flasks of tepid coffee in a windowless conference room – though, at times, we all have to do a bit of that. All industries are full of myriad formal and informal shared-interest groups and societies. These range from charities and volunteering to sports teams and professional bodies. And if the group doesn't exist for your personal passion, why not set it up?

All these are ways of connecting with people beyond your day-to-day, and broadening your personal and professional horizons. It takes a little effort, but the time invested pays off handsomely in multiple unexpected ways.

And you never know. One day, you might find you enjoy it.

CHAPTER 10

A Meetings Revolution

The executive summary of a 2017 article in the *Harvard Business Review* entitled 'Stop the Meeting Madness' began as follows:

> *Many executives feel overwhelmed by meetings, and no wonder: On average, they spend nearly 23 hours a week in them, up from less than 10 hours in the 1960s. What's more, the meetings are often poorly timed, badly run, or both.*
>
> *We can all joke about how painful they are . . . but that pain has real consequences for teams and organizations. Every minute spent in a wasteful meeting eats into solo work that's essential for creativity and efficiency. Chopped-up schedules interrupt deep thinking, so people come to work early, stay late, or use weekends for quiet time to concentrate. And dysfunctional meeting behaviors are associated with lower levels of market share, innovation, and employment stability.*

Gulp.

The situation since the pandemic has only become worse. Far from being freed by the mostly welcome advent of hybrid working, increased home working appears to have come with a significant downside for many – an even greater deluge of meetings. If we have been liberated from the scourge of presenteeism by Microsoft Teams, we have (as if to compensate) been further shackled by the tyranny of Microsoft Outlook. If you're reading this on the way to work, to an interview, during your lunch break or on a plane, the chances are that you'll be in a meeting very soon. What is to be done?!

Meetings matter, so let's do them better

Meetings come in all different shapes and sizes: virtual and in-person, on-site and off-site, formal and informal, intimidating and light-hearted. They are where cultures are shaped, problems solved, actions taken and relationships strengthened. At least, that's what they should be for.

Meetings are the basic building blocks of how organisations work. Yet they also impose a terrible tyranny that can blight our working days. Occasionally, a billionaire pipes up and tells us that if we don't need to be in a meeting, or think it's irrelevant to us, then the answer is to just stand up and leave. This is obviously terrible advice if you're not a billionaire (though we'd all love to be able to follow it from time to time). But the problem isn't meetings per se; it is that too many are badly run and there are far too many of them clogging up our diaries.

I have come to believe that the easiest, most effective and powerful change that all organisations could make which would transform their culture, their productivity and their employee engagement would be to have fewer, better meetings.

If everybody who ever put a meeting in our diaries simply abided by the following rules, then there would be no need for the rest of this chapter. That it remains is because the vast majority don't. However, henceforth, none of those should be the meetings you're responsible for.

Running great meetings requires no particular talent. Imagine the difference it would make if they were all efficient and effective. Sometimes a great and successful career involves dreaming impossible dreams. This is not such a case. Everybody can do this right now.

If you are responsible for a meeting, these are the four questions you should ask. All are easy, but commonly not done well. And if a thing that requires no talent is often done poorly, there is a ready opportunity for you to stand out from the crowd.

The four As* of great meetings

*and one P

1. Aim

What is the purpose and objective of the meeting?

Always state the aim in bold at the top of the agenda, or establish it clearly in the meeting invite. The implicit question here is whether you need a meeting at all. If everybody asked this one question, we'd all have far fewer meetings roadblocking our days, and would consequently all be both happier and more productive.

If you do need a meeting, a clear aim (understood by all attendees) will ensure it is more efficient in its use of time and more effective in achieving its goals.

Never title a meeting 'catch-up'. We've all done it, but it's lazy. It's an example of a clogging-up meeting; one of those meetings you (and therefore presumably everybody else) assume you can turn up late to, doze through, check your emails during and just generally behave in ways that you shouldn't. It doesn't signal action. It suggests an hour of unstructured filler.

2. Agenda

Always circulate the agenda at least twenty-four hours in advance, so attendees have time to give thought to the subject and their section, where relevant. Include:

- The aim, in bold, at the top of the page
- The location and time of the meeting
- The person who will be leading the meeting
- The points to be covered – with names against them if possible
- A list of the attendees and their job titles
- Any advance material attendees are expected to read through

These are all obvious good practice, but are so often forgotten, especially for meetings that are seen as less important, that are informal or happen regularly. Yet these are often the meetings that are the most inefficient and poorly run, the meetings that clog up our diaries, and that are most in need of a more disciplined approach.

3. Attendees

Think carefully about who should be invited.

It is a little depressing, but important to acknowledge, that sometimes meeting attendance is an exercise in office politics. Nevertheless, if our objective is fewer, better meetings, then collectively we must be more disciplined about who we invite.

A good rule of thumb is to only invite people if they have a specific role. This doesn't mean they have to be responsible for a defined section of the meeting, but it does mean there has to be a good reason for why they are there. More tightly controlled lists of attendees will likely lead to fewer meetings, and improve the quality of those that remain.

Similarly, if people are invited, they should be expected to actively participate. A personal bugbear is senior people who make a point of bringing junior people to meetings but give no thought to their role and who consequently sit through the whole meeting without speaking. This is bad for their confidence and their profile, and unnecessarily blocks up their diary.

Do not sit through a meeting without contributing to it, and do not invite people to meetings if you do not help them to contribute. We return to this later in the chapter.

4. Action

The most important part of any meeting is that there is a clear summary of actions, agreed before it concludes. This should include the following:

- The decisions that were taken
- The actions that were agreed upon
- The names of those responsible for relevant next steps
- Deadlines for the completion of relevant next steps
- The date of the next meeting, along with a list of expected attendees

The chair of the meeting (see below) must ensure that these details are captured before the meeting concludes.

Very few meetings need detailed minutes. They are time-consuming to produce and almost never read. However, all formal meetings and important informal meetings need the actions to be written down and circulated to the attendees – and any others who need to be informed, even if they weren't at the meeting. This should be done within twenty-four hours.

Before every meeting, it should be made clear who will be responsible for writing and circulating the meeting actions. Typically, this should be the most junior person in the room, unless there is a specific reason for it not to be. This is not demeaning. On the contrary, it is a critical step in our professional development, affording junior colleagues a clear and meaningful role. They should capture actions, ask for clarification if necessary, read them back to the room at the meeting's conclusion, then transcribe and circulate them. Meeting reports are a great way for junior staff to quickly begin to understand the business, its challenges, and gain exposure to key people. If this is you, make it your role.

Punctuality

Our most valuable resource is our time. Being late is profoundly disrespectful. Meetings should start on time. For meetings I run, I start on time with whoever is in the room, irrespective of those who are late. If someone is more than five minutes late, they are told not to come at all – unless they have let the group know in advance. It's everybody's time that is otherwise wasted. Punctuality is a key cultural behaviour every team should adopt. Frustration down, efficiency up; better meetings all round.

This is a relatively easy rule to impose (and follow) if you're senior, more difficult if you're junior. But being on time should always be your top priority, regardless of whatever else is happening. And on time means being five minutes early. If you know in advance that's going to be difficult for you, let the chair know; it's perfectly acceptable, unless you are habitually late, which leaves a terrible impression.

Another often overlooked problem with regards to punctuality is meetings overrunning, either because they started late or because they are poorly run. It is the chair's job to ensure the meeting finishes on time and that the agenda is managed throughout to ensure this is the case.

If you're running a meeting, ensure that it starts on time and finishes on time.

How to lead a meeting well

As we've established, leadership matters. It's the difference between things being done well and badly. The same applies to meetings.

A well-run meeting needs somebody to lead it. This is usually the person who has called the meeting and has circulated the agenda. It does not always need to be the most senior person in the room.

If you are leading it, you should:

- Ensure there is a well-prepared agenda circulated in advance.
- Sit in a place that signifies you're in charge. This will typically be at the head of the table or in the middle of the side facing the door if the table is rectangular. On a circular table it is less obvious (deliberately – that's the point of round tables) but the key position is typically one facing the door. In a company I once ran, we put a red chair into every meeting room for the person in charge. It had a powerful effect, signalling that a chairperson was needed for every meeting and reminding those in the room of that person's role and the importance of running meetings properly.

- Ensure that the meeting runs to time and that each of the points on the agenda is given sufficient space for discussion. If it becomes apparent that this isn't going to happen, do not allow the meeting to simply drag on. Instead, pause and agree with the room which points will be dropped from the agenda to be discussed at a later date, or can be covered by a smaller group offline.
- Always start with the most important topics to ensure they are given enough time to be concluded.
- Summarise actions and decisions. Ensure these are agreed in the room before the meeting concludes. If they are not, agree what to do next in order to reach a decision. Ensure that actions are captured and circulated.
- Finish on time.

Balancing voices

A critical role for the chair of a meeting is to ensure that the conversation in the room represents a fair balance of opinions. This is a polite way of saying: make sure everybody behaves well and that everybody's voice gets heard.

People behave badly in meetings, often without realising it. Chairing a meeting doesn't only involve sending an email in advance and clinking your teaspoon on a glass at the start. It is an active role focused on ensuring that the conversation around the table is inclusive, relevant and respectful. Anybody who has spent time in meetings knows this very often isn't the case. We're all familiar with the archetypes: The Loudmouth, The Complainer,

The Rambler, The Sulker, The Emailer, The Whisperer, The Interrupter, The Cynic, The Devil's Advocate (a personal pet peeve).

Those who talk for too long must be politely cut short; those who drift from the subject must be returned to the agenda; and those who interrupt or talk over others, asked to wait. Cynical voices need to be balanced to avoid them hijacking the discussion. A good chair draws everybody into the conversation and reads the room continuously to see how people are reacting. Do they appear hurt, angry, upset or disconnected? The chair must take note of who's speaking, how things are being said and whether people are listening to each other.

Quiet voices and silent people must be actively drawn into the conversation. If somebody has been invited to attend the meeting, then they should be heard and treated with respect. The chair must ensure this is the case. In a well-run meeting, the chair is an active rather than a passive participant, both in terms of the meeting's content and the behaviour of attendees.

Virtual meetings

These days, a large number of meetings are held entirely online. In general, the principles of a good meeting still hold. They need an aim and an agenda, they need a chair and they need defined actions at their conclusion. However, there are some specific behaviours you and your team should observe for these meetings to run well, especially if you wish to be seen as a professional and active participant.

- To ensure the meeting starts on time, log in five minutes early and wait to be let into the virtual room, then put yourself on mute. Don't wait until the exact time that the meeting is due to start before logging in.

- Your camera should be on unless there is good reason for it not to be. Your contributions will carry more weight if people can see you. And visibility is very important to your career progress.
- Think about your background. If you don't have a suitable one at home, either blur the background or choose a preset; they're so ubiquitous nobody even notices them any more. Calls from hotel rooms are a particular watch-out. An unmade bed or half-eaten tray of food on the floor in the background doesn't send the right signals to other attendees.
- Think about what you're wearing. I make no judgement about what's right or wrong – I'll leave that to you. But whatever it is, wear it consciously.
- If there are more than a handful of attendees, mute your microphone while others speak.

The role of the chair is arguably even more important for virtual meetings than in-person ones, because it is far more difficult to read people's body language online, and harder to politely interrupt those who talk too much or veer from the agenda.

In-person meetings are unquestionably preferable if difficult or important topics are to be covered. Virtual meetings are perfectly acceptable for most everyday situations. However, if at all possible, avoid meetings that are part virtual and part in-person, especially if the topic is important. The mix of the two is complicated, and they are often deeply unsatisfactory.

Speaking up

We've all been there, in the middle of a long meeting, listening to and watching our elders (although not necessarily betters) endlessly debate some topic. We watch the conversation go back and forth, the whole time with a comment or question burning to get out. We open our mouth, poised to speak, then close it – the opportunity never quite seems to come. Meanwhile, nobody pays us any attention; the chair isn't chairing anything but their WhatsApp chat. Eventually, the conversation moves on and the moment is lost. Or worse. Somebody else says the exact same thing we were thinking and everybody immediately remarks on what a good contribution it was. And we fume in the corner.

If you recognise the feeling of being unable to speak, don't be too hard on yourself. It happens to everybody. It happened to me on occasion, even once I'd become a CEO. Sometimes, there just isn't room for another voice. Nevertheless, having a role in meetings is about more than just your ego. Visibility is really important to your career, and meetings offer a relatively easy and frequent opportunity to be seen and heard. Therefore, it is important you make the most of these opportunities.

Remember that there is no correlation between being loud and opinionated, and being interesting or insightful. Sometimes the most powerful voices in a room are those who say the least – people who have listened carefully to the discussion before making a couple of insightful observations. In a noisy room, being quiet and concise can make you stand out.

If you have been invited to a meeting, you should contribute if possible. If you find that difficult sometimes, here are four straightforward things you can do right now that are an easy and effective fix.

1. Ask for a defined role

The most effective way to make sure that you're a part of the conversation is to have a section of the agenda that is your responsibility. This guarantees you a clear role in the meeting. It can't always happen, but asking for it isn't as difficult as it may seem.

The best way is to discuss it with the chair (or your boss) beforehand. This requires a little vulnerability and honesty, but everybody is familiar with the feeling. You're not alone.

It could be quite a small role, perhaps as little as presenting a single slide in the middle of somebody else's presentation, but it's enough for you to establish yourself in the room and build your confidence. Like everything else, the more you do it, the easier it becomes – and your role will expand as your confidence grows, and the confidence others have in you increases.

2. Prepared questions

If you do not have a defined role, then you can use this technique in every meeting, big and small. It's one of the more useful pieces of advice I've ever been given: *Before the meeting prepare ten generic questions that are adaptable to most situations.*

You can do this yourself, or ask an AI like ChatGPT. Write the questions down in the back of your daybook and once in the meeting you can tweak them to suit the situation.

You can then recycle these for every meeting. Once you build confidence, you'll hardly need them. This is such a simple fix that I suggest you do it right now.

3. Speak early

The longer you sit silent in a meeting, the harder it can be to speak. Conversely, once you have contributed, you immediately relax and feel more confident. It's just getting past that first hurdle.

As a rule of thumb, I would suggest you try to contribute within the first quarter of the meeting. It doesn't have to be anything profound. Most things that are said in meetings aren't, so don't set yourself too high a bar. The pre-prepared questions will really help here. It could be as simple as asking a question of clarification. The point is to establish yourself as an active rather than passive participant early on – in your own head as much as anybody else's.

Of course, this requires common sense. If the first hour is your CEO presenting – perhaps let them finish first.

4. Preparation is king

Preparation is the secret to confidence in many situations at work. Those people who make it look easy – the chances are they have prepared, even if you don't see them do it. It's easy and effective.

The more knowledgeable you feel, the greater your confidence and the more useful your contribution will be to the meeting – a virtuous circle. Speaking up is a good idea only if what you have to say is relevant, and the best contribution anybody can make to a meeting is to be able to bring something to the discussion that nobody else can.

Many people turn up to meetings having done little preparation, so if you have done your homework you'll immediately stand out. The objective is not to be an expert, but rather to bring an informed perspective to the room. Speaking from a position of knowledge will both increase your confidence and add gravitas to your contribution.

When meetings go bad

I've worked with enough people to know that many will read this chapter and nod their way through it while thinking there's little new here for them. However, knowing is not the same as doing. Everybody can always do better and, in my experience, it is often those who are the most confident who would most benefit from a little self-reflection. That might even be you.

If you can say you've never . . .

- Turned up late without good reason or explanation
- Talked over others
- Interrupted – especially somebody you consider junior to you
- Failed to ensure everybody is participating and engaged
- Failed to circulate a clear agenda
- Monopolised the discussion
- Been disrespectful in language, tone or gesture
- Ignored others
- Allowed a discussion (or even a whole meeting) to drift
- Lost your temper
- Repeatedly checked your devices, sent emails or messages
- Had side conversations
- Arrived unprepared

. . . then I don't believe you. We've all done all of them.

Sometimes the quickest way to get to good behaviours is to simply be more aware of their opposites. Swimming pools like to list all the things that are forbidden. A whole generation of British schoolchildren grew up being told off for 'bombing', and wondering what 'petting' was and why it was banned (if you're old enough, you'll remember).

What if the easiest and quickest way to improve the quality of all your meetings was to simply create the meeting equivalent and attach it to the walls of every meeting room? Or even the back of every agenda?

It'll make people laugh and is a gentle, non-threatening truth-joke to start every meeting. Would it be transformational? Perhaps not. But given the tyrannical hold meetings have over our working lives, it's worth a try.

Transformative meetings

Being busy is not the same as being effective, nor is it the same as working hard. Meetings clog up our day, and many of them are poorly run with little forethought given to the agenda or attendees, nor are they concluded with clear and agreed actions. They are part of a cyclical process that moves pieces around without ever moving anything forwards.

To make ourselves more productive, and to reduce the corrosive effects that stress and over-work have on our lives, we need to free ourselves from the tyranny of bad meetings. This means attending fewer meetings. And it means that those that remain in our diaries must become more disciplined and more effective.

Even a 20 per cent improvement means you may get a whole day back every week. For free. Time and energy to think, to do your actual job, to pick your kids up from school.

You can't always influence how others behave, but when it comes to great meetings, you can make sure you play your part.

CHAPTER 11

Writing Compelling Presentations

I vividly recall the most terrifying presentation I ever took part in – and I wasn't even speaking. Indeed, nobody could see me at all.

It was a meeting the entire company had sweated over for months, the business lurching to-and-fro like a galleon in a storm. I had no speaking part, nor was I even visible to the audience, but my role, explained to me in painstaking detail by the CEO (who'd never spoken to me before), was critical. As the meeting opened, I was frozen with fear.

It was an era we will call BPP, or Before Power Point. Every image had been converted the night before onto a 35mm slide to be projected through an aperture at the back of the boardroom. This may be utterly incomprehensible if you're below a certain age – if so, simply be thankful you will forever be spared this ordeal.

In preparation, each slide had to be held to the light so you could see what was on it and inserted in the correct orientation, back to front and upside-down, into a carousel. Each carousel held approximately forty slides and for this meeting there were around 120 slides, so three carousels.

Thirty years after the moon landings, this was the pinnacle of presentation technology.

Being responsible for the machine's operation was a fever dream. The projection room was (necessarily) unlit and (unnecessarily) un-air-conditioned. The meeting was due to last two hours, but I had to be in-situ well before. My duties were as follows. Load each carousel onto the projector and ensure it started in the correct position so that slide number one rather than slide twenty-three appeared first; to click the machine forward at a predetermined signal from the room; if a slide had been put in the wrong way (resulting in the on-screen image being upside down or back to front), to stop the machine, remove the slide, re-orient it and re-insert; if a slide jammed (a frequent occurrence) unjam it; to change the carousels at the appropriate point; to ensure the machine remained in focus.

Throughout the whole process, I had to peer through the aperture to ensure all was as it should be and to look out for any secret signals from the team.

It was one of those jobs where, if you do it well, everybody forgets you were there and consequently leaves for the after-meeting drinks without you. While, if you screw up, it's the worst day of your career to date (and possibly for many years to come). And the opportunities to screw up were manifold. The sum of all fears, one spoken of in hushed tones by us projection technicians, the projection apocalypse, was the dropped carousel. All forty carefully arranged slides (in order and orientation) scattered across the darkened floor of the projection room, to all intents and purposes resulting in the termination of the meeting.

It remains the most stressful presentation of my life. Compared to it, all others have been a walk in the park. Fortunately, on this occasion, no major disasters befell me and a small enough number of minor problems that they fell easily within the margin for error. As a result, at the meeting's conclusion I was in the happy position of simply being left behind by mistake when the rest of the team went out to celebrate.

I have spent large parts of my career working in advertising agencies whose stock-in-trade is presentations. Advertising agencies love giving presentations. They give them to themselves, their clients, their bosses, journalists, potential clients, recruiters, intermediaries, their employees, each other, their owners and many others, whether the recipients want them or not. I have therefore been fortunate in two ways. Familiarity has partly anaesthetised me to the fear of standing and speaking before an audience (although not entirely), and I have also been able to learn from some people who are very good at writing and giving presentations (the two are not the same thing) and some people who are terrible at both.

This chapter and the next are the sum of what I have learned and form two halves of a no-bullshit toolkit that will make everybody better at writing great presentations and speaking in public.

PowerPoint et al

These days, nearly all presentations are made using PowerPoint. A few creative types use Keynote – and even more exotic platforms are available. Mostly, however, PowerPoint is perfectly adequate. People moan about it, but it is just a tool – as good or as bad as its user.

Golden Rule number one is to know how to use it. It's very easy; you don't need to be taught. If you're not familiar with it, simply open it up and get going as you would with any other common-or-garden piece of software – just don't wait until an hour before the meeting to do so. You don't need to be an expert. Competence will suffice.

It amazes me how many people, junior and senior, cannot use

PowerPoint. Some, especially senior people, see it as a mark of honour; perhaps they consider it beneath them. Yet being able to use the tools well means being able to create better presentations. Not least because by having at least a basic understanding of how the software works, you retain the option of making corrections yourself, which at critical moments may be very important indeed.

If you're serious about being at your best when you get up to speak, then learning the basics of PowerPoint matters. Every audience, every room, every brief is different. Even if you are 100 per cent certain the night before, when you arrive on the morning you may change your mind. You might want to add, remove, amend or (a regular occurrence) fix a typo. You might spot that the client's name has been spelt incorrectly. The best presenters sweat the small stuff and, if necessary, can fix it themselves.

This is not an argument for having to create every presentation yourself. It is a warning of the perils of not being able to use the tool properly should the situation demand it – as well as a reminder of the indispensable nature of those who, especially in moments of stress and crisis, are able to do so.

How to write a great presentation

All great presentations start with a simple question:

What is your objective?

In the world of business, typical answers might include:

- To persuade a prospective client to work with you
- To explain to your audience the status of a particular project and gain their support

- To pitch for an increased budget for your project
- To get approval for the coming year's business plan
- To launch a new project
- To help your audience better understand a particular topic or project
- To debrief research findings

Even the most mundane of presentations should have an objective – something the presenter would like to achieve by its conclusion. This may seem obvious, but one of the most common reasons presentations are poor is because their originator hasn't taken the time to consider their true objective. They might have too many, making it difficult for the audience to work out what is being asked of them – or conversely, no clearly defined objective at all, which has the same effect.

The first rule is to have only one per presentation and to make sure that you and your team are clear on what it is. If the topic is large, there may well be different sections or chapters, but these should all form part of a single, coherent whole.

A clear objective is your ally

A clear objective is your guide and editor. It keeps you pointing in the right direction, provides the glue that coheres your argument and helps you decide what must be included and what can be left out.

Bad presentations do none of these things. They are often too long, unstructured and contain too many different ideas. Consequently, each slide, whether beautifully designed or not, slips like wet soap from the memory. Your time and the audience's wasted.

Creating and delivering presentations are a means to an end. Be clear on your objective before you begin and you'll get better results. Too often, the presenter makes their audience guess what this might be. Don't. Always tell your audience upfront what it is. Be big, bold and clear. No frills, no filler.

For example, my objective for this chapter is:

To provide a no-bullshit toolkit that will make everybody better at writing presentations.

Accomplished presenters may not feel the need to be as blunt and direct as this. However, all great craftsmen start with a deep understanding of the basic principles; later, having learned their trade, they can decide which to discard, which to re-imagine and which to keep. My advice when writing presentations is: if in doubt, spell your objective out. Your audience will thank you.

Put your audience first

In the old days, before PowerPoint, when people gave a business presentation they would arrive with physical copies of their slides – usually cardboard-framed acetates which were placed on overhead projectors. Before they began, the presenter would take the stack of slides from their bag and place them in a pile next to the projector, giving the audience an immediate visual guide to how long the presentation was going to be.

I distinctly remember sitting in trepidation waiting for the big reveal: *How long were we going to be there?* Then the sick feeling in my stomach as a six-inch mountain of slides was deposited on the desk, the dusty, mute eye of the projector waiting to begin its painful work. Tellingly, I can remember that feeling, yet not a single one of the names, faces, subjects or objectives.

PowerPoint allows us to hide the number of slides we're about to present, but it's a good exercise to imagine if, next to you, there was a pile of your slides that the audience could see. How would they feel? How would you feel if you were them?

Because preparing and delivering presentations can be a stressful business, too often the audience is forgotten in the speaker's desire to just get it done; to hit their key points, to remember their lines and handover points, and to stay on time. And even then, many don't manage it. The presenter puts their own needs first, when in reality it's about the audience – not you. They are why you are there. It is them you are trying to persuade.

Once you're clear on your objective, you must put yourselves in the shoes of the people you are talking to. Why are they there, what do they want, what might their preconceptions or anxieties or deadlines be?

For you to achieve *your* objective, you have to give serious thought to *theirs*.

A simple structure

How we write is a personal choice. Some people write in order to clarify their thoughts, others need their ideas to be clear before they can begin to write. Some need a weight of data and facts before being able to formulate a recommendation, some have strong instincts and use data and research to torture-test their ideas. None are wrong, none better, simply different. All good presentations, however, should have a clear structure.

As with any rules, they are there to be broken – but if you do, take care not to lose yourself or your audience:

Remember the old maxim:

- Start: Tell them what you're about to tell them

- Middle: Tell them
- End: Tell them what you told them

It is timeless and effective; everybody knows it. And yet most don't follow it.

Here is a simple six-point structure to use when preparing any presentation.

1. Introduction

- Always have a title. If possible, relate this to your objective.
- Introduce yourself and any other people who will be presenting.
- If the audience doesn't know you or your team, consider leaving picture cards on the table with names, job titles and photos. People will forget these details if you rely on a quick verbal introduction alone. Even better, leave a group photo – it's amazing the power this has to make you look like a tight team.

2. Contents

Some presenters consider the inclusion of a contents page overly formal, and in certain situations I agree. In short presentations, they're usually unnecessary. However, in long presentations, or in those that contain multiple sections, it's a good idea to provide the audience with an outline of what you're about to share with them, including:

- An overview of the presentation's structure
- Who will be speaking in each section

- How long each section will take
- Where any breaks in the presentation will be
- When questions will be invited

3. Objective

Be clear on the objective of your presentation. Examples might be:

- 'Today we wish to persuade you of . . .'
- 'We're going to show you a brilliant idea which will . . .'
- 'Our proposal today is that . . .'
- 'We wish to raise [insert amount] of funding for a project that will achieve . . .'
- 'We're going to transform your understanding of . . .'
- 'We're going to celebrate a fantastic year where we achieved . . .'

It can be as straightforward or as poetic as you wish. But don't make your audience guess. At least, don't make them guess unless it is a conscious and deliberate tactic – and if it is, ensure your presentation is designed such that they guess correctly.

Sometimes, you may be responding to a brief or to a specific question. If so, include it. This has the dual benefit of demonstrating that you have read the brief and reminding your audience what it was they had asked of you. It is surprising how often this leads to an immediate debate, as the audience themselves has forgotten what it was they asked or discover they are not in full agreement with each other. Many is the meeting I've sat in where the first thirty minutes ends up being the client debating their own brief.

4. Chapters and signposts

Chapters and their subsections are the meat of the presentation.

- In most presentations, you'll require chapters or section headings. Think of these as signposts that point the way for the audience. Use them to break your argument into bitesize pieces, making it easier to digest. Some presenters may wish to invite questions at the end of each chapter.
- Chapters shouldn't just be numbered but given their own clear title. These can be considered the skeleton of your presentation from which the flesh is hung – sorry if that's a bit yuck. Some presenters structure them in such a way that if the rest of the slides were removed these alone would be sufficient for them to tell the story.

In practice, good presenters start with many more slides than they will eventually use, and through an iterative process gradually pare them back, leaving a skeleton of chapter slides to guide the audience, trusting themselves to flesh out the rest as they present. The trick is to find a complementary balance between what is shown and what is said.

It is important to note here that just as it's possible to be too long-winded and include too many slides, it is also possible to be too assumptive and sparse in your visual aids, making it unnecessarily difficult for your audience to follow your thread. Ultimately, the ability to find the Goldilocks zone, not too many and not too few, comes with experience, not just of your own preference but the ability to judge an audience's needs.

5. Numbers, data and sources

Often you will have a set of hard facts that you must communicate in your presentation – e.g., financial performance data, productivity reports, research results, customer churn etc. Their delivery may sometimes be the presentation's objective, while at other times data such as this may be structural support around your central theme. Either way, make sure you use it in such a way as to achieve your desired results. Remember:

- If data is required, it must be shown on screen and not just delivered verbally.
- Always pre-digest data for your audience. Too often, data is presented as a blizzard of numbers, graphs, icons and arrows – making it all but impossible for the audience to understand, or sometimes even see, the point being made. If this happens, you lose the room.
- Do the analysis for them. Show only the most salient points that support your insights and conclusions. Ensure it is clear which points matter most and that the audience remembers and understands the bits you need them to.
- If necessary, you can always include more detail in the appendix, on a micro-site, or as a take-away.
- Know your material. Just because you don't include every detail on screen, you have to be familiar with all of it – you never know what questions you're going to be asked.

- Always include sources for any data, quotes, research information, competitor information and so on. I have known people make them up; I wouldn't recommend it.

6. Conclusion

This is the last thing your audience will hear. Therefore, make it matter: tell them what you've told them. And ask them for what you want.

Your conclusion should not be anything new, but simply the end point of a thread that begins with your objective and runs through the various arguments of your presentation. It should be short, punchy and something they've already heard. There should be no surprises – if you've done a good job, the audience should be able to write it themselves.

By this point the audience should not be simply thankful it is finally over (don't laugh, this is very common). Instead, they should be clear on your objective, the salient points of your argument and your conclusion(s).

Ideally, they will also now be in wholehearted agreement with you, but life is rarely so straightforward. You cannot control the audience's response, but you can control how good a case you make. This should be sufficiently tight and clear that, agree or not, any person watching your presentation could summarise your argument themselves.

From good to great

Now you know the rules for writing an effective presentation, here's how you ensure it's a great and memorable one.

Fermentation

The more you become familiar with a task, the quicker and more proficient you will become, but even so, if you leave writing a new presentation until the night before, the odds are it will be rubbish.

This is a book for the real world and you will rarely have as much time as you'd like to work on your presentation, but if it's important then you need to get started on it as early as possible. Get to a rough first draft quickly, then allow it time to ferment. Most presentations are not huge set-piece events, but even mundane ones can be made better and more effective if you buy yourself time to think.

Frequently, I have looked back at important presentations several weeks after the event and been surprised at their length. In the intervening period, my mind had distilled it to the key points, the best slides and the pivotal arguments. On reopening it I have discovered large sections where I think, why did we include that?

I could probably cut 25 per cent of any presentation I've ever done after a few weeks of not thinking about it. This is fermentation in action. Time makes presentations crisper, sharper and more succinct – so if you have time, use it.

Once you have a draft, present it out loud, either on your own or with others. As soon as you do, you'll begin to discover gaps and where there is fat that can be cut. This will begin to sharpen your argument, your structure and your use of visual aids.

As short as possible and no shorter

Most presentations can be improved by making them shorter. In his book, *Everything I Know About Life I Learned from PowerPoint*, the strategy guru Russell Davies describes a study published in 2021 in *Nature* where people were asked to correct an unstable Lego tower.

> *. . . people immediately think about adding bricks, not removing them, even when taking them away would have been quicker and easier.*

We've all built a wobbly leaning tower of a presentation, with annexes bolted on here and there to try to keep it upright. And we've all had the misfortune of sitting through them.

It is always possible to say more – and, if you're the master of your subject, to say many more interesting and exciting things. Your audience may even be quite happy for you to do so. However, beyond a certain point, the more you tell people, the less they remember, and the more likely you become to obscure your central objective and argument.

When judging the length of a presentation, a reliable guide is that it is rare for somebody to spend less than sixty seconds on each slide. And often people spend far longer. Therefore, if somebody turns up with a sixty-slide presentation and tells you that they'll get through it in thirty minutes (it happens all the time) – don't believe them. It's more likely to take two hours. And when timing your own presentation, don't kid yourself.

A good rule of thumb is that you should not keep your audience seated in the same place without a break for more than ninety minutes. If necessary, segment your presentation into sixty-minute sections, and schedule breaks in between. That way you keep their attention and increase your chances of achieving your objective.

It is rare that an audience's response is: *I wish that guy could have gone on for longer.*

So don't.

The Fremantle Doctor

I find the names of winds particularly romantic: the Sirocco, the Mistral, the Chinook, the Khamsin. My favourite, however, is the Fremantle Doctor. I've never been to Perth, but I imagine its cooling airs curling in from the Indian Ocean. Mostly however, as a cricket fan, I love the idea of its hidden hand correcting the bowlers' swinging actions and confounding the batsmen at the city's (in) famous WACA ground. And, like the Western Australian bowlers on their legendary pitch, all great presentations benefit from a little doctoring.

Structuring presentations is an art, not a science. Once you have a first draft, print it out as individual slides, lay it out on a large table or pin it to a wall to review it in its entirety. This is a great way to make sure the flow of your argument works for others as well as you, to identify gaps and begin to cut what is superfluous. You should repeat this process through the presentation's iterations. If there is more than one speaker, each should take part in this process.

Once you're nearly done, get a doctor in. Find somebody who hasn't been involved and take them through the presentation. Do it properly – tell as well as show. Fresh eyes and ears will bring a new perspective, especially if you have been working on it for a long time. Familiarity may not have bred contempt, but it is likely to have bred fatigue.

Some presenters don't like doing this – and I understand why. Too many new opinions late in the day can hinder more than they help, but a sensitive listener will understand how to give constructive input. It is also a good idea to give them a brief, outlining specifically where you'd like them to focus. With forty-eight hours to go, you don't want a whole new theme, but you should welcome suggestions on how to improve the one you have.

Simple rules for designing a presentation

This is not a book on design, and I'm not a designer, but designing good PowerPoint slides is not difficult to do well. Yet it is even easier to do badly – and when preparing a presentation, design matters.

A great presentation is not a speech; it is a blend of what is said and what is shown, which together help the audience follow your argument. Too many words on too many slides leave no space for the personality of the presenter and risks obscuring your key message in a blizzard of details. Too few words on too few slides risk making it difficult for the audience to follow. What is said and what is read should dovetail and reinforce, rather than repeat and overlap. The slides are there for both the audience and the presenter, to keep both on track.

It is very important that you pay attention to how your slides look. PowerPoint has made creating presentations a lot easier than it used to be, but it has not necessarily made them look any better; in fact, it seems to have made many of them worse.

A cheat code

I hate badly designed presentations. I know what I like and I know what I don't, but I lack the design skills to get from the latter to the former. Interestingly, many actual designers are also not very good at designing presentations, though I have come to the conclusion that this may be a deliberate tactic to avoid ever being asked to do it again.

However, these days help is at hand. It is possible to find high-quality presentation templates online (the ones that come with PowerPoint and Keynote aren't much good). As is reasonable, the ones you have to pay for are usually better than those that are free, but if it matters it's worth spending the money. Personally, I have used Envato Elements in the past, but many other sites are available.

Ten-point presentation checklist

1. *Minimum 60 seconds per slide*
   Assume each slide will take a *minimum* of 60 seconds to present. Most take longer.

2. *Chapters*
   Break the presentation into clearly titled (sign-posted) chapters which cumulatively form the skeleton of your argument.

3. *Focus*
   Make only one point per slide – and be clear what it is.

4. *Keep slides simple*
   - Use visual hierarchy to emphasise key points.
   - Limit the use of text as far as possible.
   - Avoid clutter.
   - Remember, slides are visual aids, not a script.

5. *Avoid lists*
   Unless you're making a point that can only be done in that way.

6. *Never use:*
   - Clipart
   - Pre-set animations
   - Fonts that mimic handwriting
   - Slide transitions

   All of these always look dreadful.

7. *Consistent design*
   Use a single consistent theme, colour palette and limit fonts to three (in reality there's rarely a need for more than two).

8. *Avoid bullet points*
   A presentation is not an email or a book. If you have to use bullet points, ruthlessly edit them.

9. *Use pictures to tell stories*
   A picture can tell a thousand words and be far more memorable. But . . .

   The right words are always better than the wrong picture.

   Make sure the visual aids complement rather than confuse. I've seen presentations where the speaker has used a series of increasingly esoteric visuals that were so random, they simply distracted and quietly amused the audience. This is not the desired response. Unless of course it is.

10. *Readability*
    - Ensure the style of font is easy to read.
    - Ensure the colours used provide enough contrast to be legible.
    - Ensure the type is large enough to be read by the audience.

One of the most memorable presentations I ever sat in was a quarterly financial review (yes, really). These are not my favourite meetings, mostly because the people presenting consider them to be a chore that they'd rather not be dragged through – and I, having a short attention span, want to get to the actions and rapidly past the filler. They can become an exercise in expectation management – and patience.

In this case, the office had been struggling and had a new CEO. However, she obviously hadn't got the 'keep it dull and safe memo' and opened with a gif of a dumpster fire.

She had my attention. And, as it transpired, she also had a clear and ultimately successful plan. It was all the better for the look on the CFO's face.

CHAPTER 12

Ten Rules for Speaking in Public

For many people, standing up in front of others and speaking is a scary prospect. It's perhaps the number one work phobia, ahead even of networking. It is also true that there are those for whom the sound of their own voice is so irresistible that their audience soon finds themselves wishing they were somewhere else.

I believe speaking in public is like tiling. I can't tile, but (with apologies to those who can) I think that if you or I tiled ten bathrooms across a two-week period, by the last one we'd be able to do a pretty good job in a reasonable time. We wouldn't be experts, but it'd be okay. The reason I'm not yet competent at tiling is not because it is an innately very difficult task, it is because my opportunities to practise are very infrequent.

This does not apply to everything. We can't reach competence at a musical instrument in a two-week period. I do, however, think it's true of tiling. And it's also true of speaking in public. It is the infrequency of opportunity that means it takes a long time to build our confidence, overcome our fears and develop our skills – not the fact that it is an innately difficult task. Incidentally, I think this principle can also be applied to many other parts of our careers.

Most presentations we sit through are not very good. They are poorly constructed, poorly designed and poorly delivered. The problem is that opportunities to practise public speaking are, for many people, relatively few and far between – and with a bit of cunning can sometimes be avoided entirely. This means that it can take far longer than it should for people to become proficient. And for many roles, proficiency when speaking in public is a very useful (if not crucial) skill.

I have worked with talented people who have simply refused point-blank to speak publicly, even in relatively small meetings and for short periods of time. Ultimately, it held them back – until they overcame their fear. At the other extreme, I remember somebody who was so good at public speaking that she presented the bulk of a major strategic pitch to a large new prospect, despite being by far the most junior person in the room. She never lacked for roles in meetings and reaped the deserved rewards. If speaking in front of others makes you nervous, or even scared, there is no advice anybody can give that will completely remove these emotions. However, if you follow these ten rules, you will quickly become far more comfortable, less anxious, more confident and, most important of all, more competent when speaking in public.

You might even begin to enjoy it.

1. Progressive exposure

There is no way of over-coming presentation-a-phobia without frequent exposure.

While writing this chapter, I happened to discuss it with a newly qualified teacher. She told me that she too had initially been terrified of speaking in public but, at teacher-training college, had every day to present in front of her fellow students. What began as an ordeal had, within two weeks, become mundane. Like tiling.

Set yourself the objective of speaking in front of others ten times within the next three months. It could be as little as one slide at a time, or a five-minute section of a larger presentation. And, if you're feeling very brave, ask somebody for some feedback afterwards. Ask them to start with what you did well – the most important aspect of building confidence. This, however, is not essential. At first it is simply the progressive exposure that matters.

Opportunities to present more often may not arise unbidden; you are likely to have to hunt them out. If it scares you this requires a little courage, but I promise it's worth it. Sometimes people will say no. But if you ask, opportunities will come.

Practice is the surest way to rapidly improve and become more confident at any skill. And this is not a difficult skill to learn. You just have to make sure the gap between each occasion is short enough for you to gain the cumulative benefit. If you only present once a year, as with tiling (sorry, I'll stop soon), it's going to take a long time to improve – and every time is going to feel just like the first. Therefore, take every opportunity. Don't hide away.

This may sound like terrible advice if your main focus is to avoid having to speak in front of other people, but most business presentations and/or speeches are not the all-singing, all-dancing varieties that I focused on in the previous chapter. Mostly, they're smaller, less pressured and informal. Nevertheless, the principles stay the same. The more you practise, the more you will improve, and the less scary it will rapidly become.

2. 90 per cent preparation, 10 per cent inspiration

When it comes to speaking in public, confidence helps but only gets you so far. A confident speaker who has nothing to say, or who hasn't prepared well, is significantly less effective (and engaging) than one who is less confident but has taken a thoughtful and professional approach. Whatever your emotions about the subject, preparation should be your starting point.

Not many people can wing a presentation and do it well. Admittedly, some can, but they are rare and this is always the result of lots of unseen practice and experience. Less rare are those who *think* they can wing a presentation and do it well – they are mostly rubbish. Good presenters look fluid, spontaneous and at ease because they've prepared properly – and through trial and error have learned what kind of preparation works for them.

Do not be fooled into thinking that people who make something look easy find it easy. And don't be fooled into thinking that just because you haven't seen somebody prepare, they haven't done so. Preparation is a very personal thing, so you must listen to yourself and through trial and error discover what works for you. If you are relatively inexperienced, I suggest you start by writing out your speaking part longhand. Speaking is not prose, but this will give you a fail-safe fallback should you need it, as well as a solid starting point from which you can refine your delivery. If you feel very confident of your material, or are an experienced speaker, you may not need to do this, but do not underestimate the extent to which nerves can get in the way. There are no prizes for doing it all from memory, but there are obvious and awkward pitfalls in hoping it will just all be okay on the day, then drying up midway through your first slide. It happens.

I still always start by writing a new presentation out in a series of bullet points. Sometimes, if there is a particularly important passage, I write that out longhand to help me formulate the best way of expressing myself. As you rehearse, you will be able to make these notes shorter and shorter.

Ultimately my objective is to end up with a short list of bullet-pointed headings which act as an aide memoire when I come to speak. I have, in the past, made the mistake of abbreviating too much (and under-rehearsing) and found myself staring in incomprehension at my notes once I've stood up to speak. If I get it right, the notes never leave my pocket, but I know they're there should my mind go blank.

If you prepare properly, you'll find that your notes are a crutch that makes you feel better, but you won't actually need them. Even if I am giving a presentation I have done hundreds of times before, I always have notes somewhere to hand. I advise you also to err on the side of caution. Having a back-up plan in your pocket creates a virtuous circle – having it will make you feel more confident and therefore reduce the likelihood of you needing it. Write notes on small cards that, if necessary, you can hold while you speak. This is perfectly acceptable and not distracting for the audience.

And so what if you do use your notes. Nobody cares, and it shows that you've properly prepared.

3. Rehearse

Everybody should rehearse, at least until they become an established and confident speaker. Even then, it's startling how blank your mind can go under pressure, or how jumbled the most straightforward sentences can become.

Do not fear nerves. They're perfectly normal. They are not a sign of weakness or inexperience. I have never lost the feeling of nervousness before I present. Your breath quickens, your palms sweat; the more important the meeting, the more nervous you feel. Some of the greatest performers talk of their fear of audiences, although it's up to you if you listen to the advice Sir Laurence Olivier was given by a fellow actor: 'Take drugs, darling, we all do.'

Rehearsing develops a muscle memory; bullet-pointed notes are a confidence-building crutch to fall back on.

There is another very important reason to practise. One that applies to the confident as much as the inexperienced. Because people are often adrenaline-fuelled when they begin to speak, they lose track of time, causing them to significantly over-run. This can be a big problem for those speakers who are to follow, as well as being exhausting for the audience. Keeping track of time while you speak is very important – and easy. Use a timer on your phone if you don't wear a watch.

Public speaking isn't about remembering the words. It's about being able to communicate them clearly, concisely and within the given time, and the best way to make sure of that is to rehearse, rehearse, rehearse.

4. Be you

Often at work, we feel we have to try to be somebody that we're not. If we feel worried, we pretend to be confident; if we're unsure, we pretend to be certain; if ambivalent, we pretend to be impassioned. And sometimes a bit of bluster, optimism and confidence can carry us over the bumps we encounter from time to time. 'Fake it until you make it' works. Up to a point.

We enjoy listening to great presenters because we get to see a little of who they really are. We warm to them, we want them to win, to succeed; they are story tellers who take us on a roller-coaster journey, high and low, fast and slow, laughter and drama. They do this by sharing a little of their humanity with us.

One of the most accomplished presenters I ever had the pleasure of seeing was not grand, verbose, nor swaggering. Jon Steel became a legend in the advertising industry not just for the quality of his thinking, but for his ability to share it with his audience in a compelling and entertaining way.

In his book *Perfect Pitch*, Steel recounts a story from when he pitched for Porsche's advertising account in the US in 1993. Porsche was in deep crisis. In seven years, sales had dropped from 30,000 to just 7,000 cars – a precipitous decline by any standards. Steel ran a series of focus groups to try to get to the root of the issue.

The day of the pitch arrived and the anxious client was ushered into the boardroom of Steel's agency's San Francisco headquarters. Steel and his team had done months of meticulous work and were excited to share what they'd learned, as well as their recommendations. They had discovered that the problems Porsche faced were varied and complicated – everything from cheaper competition and poor marketing to issues with the product portfolio and economic pressures. However, once introductions had been concluded and coffees poured, Steel made the client an unexpected offer.

He stood and held a single piece of polyboard, its back to the client. 'You can have,' he said, 'the three-hour version, or the one-slide version.'

Steel takes up the story:

> *In one focus group, I asked a group of non-Porsche owners to imagine that they were sitting in their car at a stop light. A cartoon drawing showed them sitting in their car, looking over as a Porsche 911 drew up alongside them. From their car emanated an empty thought bubble . . . I asked them to write their thoughts in the bubble.*

It was one such image that Steel held.

Which option do you think the clients chose?

It was a courageous approach for such a high-pressure meeting. But when he turned the board around, he was able to encapsulate the brand's challenge without saying a word. The meeting was over almost before it had begun, and set Porsche on its way to becoming the powerhouse brand it remains to this day.

Ironically, Jon is one of the few people I would happily listen to for three hours. Audiences want to listen to human beings, not robots. If you're a little nervous, it's okay to say so. If you lose your way, it's okay to pause and check your notes – that's why they're there. If you don't know the answer to a question, it's okay to say you will think about it and respond later.

5. Build bridges with your audience

Effective speakers build bridges with their audience as Jon Steel did. It's easy to forget that they are people too, just like you. Remember, they are there because they want or need to hear what you have to say, even if sometimes it doesn't look that way.

Good presenters find ways to connect with their audience – ideally, early in their presentation. They do this by using stories to bring their presentation to life. A common way is to start with a personal anecdote or recent news story. Watch how good presenters do this – apparently spontaneously. It usually isn't spontaneous, but is a very effective way to frame their presentation, draw the audience in and immediately engage them in what they have to say.

A colleague once opened an important pitch meeting with a clip of Buzz Lightyear from *Toy Story 3*. Buzz had been inadvertently reset to the Spanish version and performs a series of seductive flamenco pirouettes around a bewildered female character (it's on YouTube; if you don't know it, hunt it out – it's very funny).

'I'm sure you'll be seeing lots of other agencies in the next two days,' he observed.

Ice broken; the competition gently put in their place.

I often speak on the subject of leadership, so I'm in the habit of screenshotting any interesting, amusing, quirky or powerful stories I see about leaders and leadership. These are a mix of news stories, interviews, quotes, cartoons, pieces of research and anything else which catches my eye. They sit in a folder on my phone. I now have quite a large and eclectic file of images, which means that when I need something to add a little colour to a presentation, I have a pool of engaging material to hand. You can use a similar approach to add texture and humanity to almost any subject. Just begin to collect stuff; today, it's easier than ever.

Of course, you may often only have a short period of time to prepare for a presentation. If you're in need of some quick inspiration, buy a couple of magazines or newspapers relevant to the subject. They'll throw up something you can use. If you find something, take the magazine into the room as a prop and read directly from it. In a world of screens and slides something physical adds texture and cut-through to your presentation. It's very simple and effective. Reliable sources include the *Harvard Business Review*, *Newsweek*, *The Spectator*, *The New Statesman*, *The Atlantic*, *Time*, *Fortune*, *Wired*, *Fast Company*, any daily newspaper and, of course, *The Economist*. And use Google and AI models like ChatGPT.

It's even more fun to try to take a reference from a less-expected source. If you're talking to CFOs, they'll sit up and pay attention if you open a copy of *Vogue* and share a snippet to illustrate a point. Try sports mags, lifestyle mags or music periodicals. Don't over-think it, but don't underestimate the power of an attention-catching opening story and a prop.

6. Be a supportive audience

I have taken part in thousands of presentations. Over time I got used to watching the room as well as the speaker. After all, it's the people in the room that we were trying to influence, so it's useful to try to gauge their response. It's a good habit to get into. I've also watched speakers, experienced and novice, as they prepare and present.

On one memorable occasion when I was a relative newbie, a colleague was presenting to a very big client. I cannot remember the subject, but I do remember that it was important enough for the business's two founders to be in the room. They made for an uncomfortable double act and my colleague was understandably nervous. After a while, the two partners began making anxious signals to her. One, with his palms flat, made 'slow down' gestures. The other, on the opposite side of the table, span his index fingers about each other, instructing her to speed up.

It's an extreme example of a phenomenon we've all experienced. For many, the people they are most nervous about speaking in front of are those who should be most on their side: their bosses.

There comes a point before a presentation where what matters most is that the team is able to focus on doing a great job with the materials they have – and to stop making changes. Last-minute interference does little to improve the overall argument, it simply stops team members being able to prepare properly. This is a very common mistake, and senior people are particularly guilty.

Rather than meddle in the details, leaders should offer support and space to those presenting. If someone is crippled by anxiety in front of their boss, it is primarily not their fault. It is a leader's responsibility to help their teams improve at this crucial skill, but also to ensure that on the occasions when they're present, they're helping rather than hindering. And it's a general principle that can be extended to everybody. If you're on the team but not presenting, help those who are by giving them the space to prepare properly. They'll love you for it.

If I'm in charge of a team I have a simple method to ensure everybody keeps to time when presenting. At the beginning of the meeting, I tell the audience and speakers that is my role and if I believe time is becoming an issue I will simply tell the presenter how long they have left. No complicated signals. Very straightforward. No ambiguity. No stress (or at least – no additional stress).

7. Prepare for questions

Questions are a crucial part of achieving your objective. They are not simply an inconvenience to be squeezed in if you have time. Unless there is a specific reason not to, always allow time for questions. As a rule of thumb, about a quarter of the allotted time is about right. Which means for an hour-long meeting, and assuming everybody is on time, you should budget as follows:

- 5 mins: Introductions and formalities
- 40 mins: Presenting
- 15 mins: Questions

You must remember that there is a big difference between a presentation that lasts fifty-five minutes and one that lasts forty minutes.

You should also try to ensure that all the most difficult questions are asked while you're still in the room. If they aren't asked, it doesn't mean they're not being thought and, even if you are unable to answer them there and then, you can at least understand what the barriers are to achieving your goal. Nobody has a monopoly on being right, and great solutions are often arrived at through the cumulative effects of thoughtful questioning and considered responses. For this reason, you should encourage difficult questions, even if you don't immediately have an answer.

The questions asked are beyond your control, but this is no reason to not prepare. Before the meeting, you should always spend a little time brainstorming possible questions and answers. This has the dual benefit of sharpening your own thinking and preparing you for what might be asked.

Handling questions is another easy skill that is so often screwed up.

As with all meetings, there should be a chair who runs the Q&A, inviting questions and indicating who should speak next. If they've done their job and have been watching the audience throughout, they may proactively ask somebody if they have a question. As chair, I would always make sure to ask the most senior person present if they had not already spoken. If people are invited to ask a question, they often do.

If you wish to give the impression of an aligned team with a clearly thought-through recommendation, the cardinal rule is that a maximum of two people should answer each question. The chair should indicate who will answer and ensure this rule is followed. The effectiveness of a team's response to an audience question is inversely proportional to the amount of people who offer an answer. The more people who answer, the less convinced the audience becomes.

The reason more than one person might jump in to answer is because they don't like the response already given and think they can say it better. This happens because the presenters believe they are required to find the 'right answer'. They are not. They are required to respond respectfully and thoughtfully. If the question is difficult, they can follow up afterwards with a more considered response.

8. Context matters

Often, you find yourself with only limited control over *where* you will be presenting. But it's uncommon for you to have none. Good presenters spend time thinking about the environment they will present in, and the extent to which they can improve the experience for the audience. For big meetings, if you can, you should dress the room. This might mean pads and pencils at every place, refreshments, flowers and a seating plan.

For many years, in important meetings, we would provide expensive patisserie or handmade chocolates, which were laid out in extravagant piles along the table in the belief that this would endear us to the audience. During one meeting, I watched whether people ate them. For nearly an hour, nobody touched the fancy cookies. I have a sweet tooth and found it a struggle to resist. Then, finally, somebody snapped and within a minute everybody (including me) had surrendered and dived in. What, I wondered afterwards, had they all been thinking about during the preceding hour? Instead of listening to our fabulously crafted presentation, had they all instead been fighting an internal battle to preserve their waistlines? I didn't want the audience wrestling to resist temptation; I wanted them thinking only of our honeyed words. The next time we offered fruit. The time after that, chopped-up fruit – turns out nobody wants to peel an orange in the middle of a presentation.

Context matters, so you should do what you can to control it. Provide refreshments and natural light. If you care where people sit, don't make them guess. Have place cards and schedule breaks. Remember: if people are distracted, feel uncomfortable, are too hot or too cold, or they need the loo, they aren't listening to you.

9. Pre-flight checks

Before a pilot takes off, they walk around the aircraft and visually assure themselves all is as it should be. It might seem slightly anachronistic in our day and age, but we should be reassured by this. Before departure, they must sign a form taking responsibility for the aircraft. Likewise, the golden rule of presenting is to always personally check your section of the presentation before you begin. Always. The one time you don't, there will be a problem and, however much you fume, it will be nobody's fault but yours.

This check must be done on the machine or platform you are due to speak from, and you must click through every slide. Do both, every time.

You'll be amazed at the capacity of both eager helpers and technology to trip you up. Fonts become corrupted, images pixelate, slides disappear or become re-ordered, deleted slides mysteriously re-appear, video files refuse to play, or the audio doesn't work. All this and more has happened to me on more occasions than I care to recall. Sometimes I checked and found out just in time. Sometimes I didn't, and suffered the consequences.

Never present from a file held in the cloud. Always have it on the machine's hard drive when presenting – never rely on meeting-room Wi-Fi connections.

If there are problems, it is far better to delay the start of the presentation while they are resolved than to discover midway through and come to a juddering halt. Aside from the effect on your audience when their name is spelt incorrectly on the first slide, small errors can be a significant distraction for you just when you need it least. Speaking in public can be stressful, and stumbling across an unexpected problem can throw a presenter completely off course, causing far more harm than the error itself.

So always check the deck!

10. Buy a f**king clicker

Remember the government's daily COVID press conferences back in 2020? Surely, it wasn't just me who was screaming 'BUY A F**KING CLICKER' at the TV as the UK's greatest scientific brains were repeatedly forced to say, 'Next slide, please,' throughout their presentations. Day after day, month after month.

How could they be so amateurish? Did they think clicking was beneath them?

Never do it.

Imagine listening to your favourite author read the climactic chapter of their greatest book, only for them to stop every sixty seconds to say, 'Next page, please.' And every now and again, 'Oh, wait, hang on, you've missed one, go back.' It happens all the time, but don't let it happen to you.

Buy a f**king clicker.

. . . and breathe

A successful presentation isn't just *what* is said, it's *how* it is said. Much of presenting well is putting the audience at ease. The more relaxed and confident you appear (even if you are a raging torrent inside), the more relaxed and happy the audience will feel. And how they feel matters to your ultimate success.

I've seen courageous presenters in important meetings admit that they feel nervous. Though I'm sure unintentionally so, it is a bold power play. The room leaned in, immediately on the speaker's side at the unexpected glimpse of vulnerability that all could empathise with.

Your audience doesn't expect perfection; they certainly don't want to be presented to by a robot. They want a real person who has prepared thoroughly, knows their subject, is sincere and cares. All of these you can do.

We are often so hyped up when we stand to speak in an important meeting that we rush headlong into the words we have prepared. But you must remember not to. If you only hold one card in your hand as you stand, write on it this:

Smile
Say hello
Tell them your first name
And breathe.

It'll relax you and it'll relax the audience.

Then begin.

Presenting – in a page (or two)

Be clear on your objective

1. Say it out loud and write it on a slide.
2. Repeat it at the conclusion, summarising, if necessary, the way(s) you have met it.

Writing and design

1. A presentation is a blend of what's shown and what's said.
2. Remember the audience – you're doing it for them, not you.
3. Chapters are signposts that provide structure.
4. Design matters. Use a simple, consistent design and an easy-to-read font.
5. One idea per slide. One slide is a minimum of 60–90 seconds.
6. Avoid bullet points, lists, clipart and fancy slide transitions.
7. For important or complicated sections, the 'Build' feature works well.
8. Pre-digest data; be clear what matters most and include only this on your slides.
9. Use pictures as well as words, but don't be too esoteric.

Preparation

1. Write your argument out longhand, then refine it into bullet points.
2. Practise out-loud – a lot.
3. Make it topical or personal to connect with your audience.
4. Get a doctor – for the slides, not you.
5. Smile; say hello; tell them your name; breathe.

Questions

1. Leave around 25 per cent of your allotted time for questions.
2. If you don't know the answer immediately, say so and respond later.
3. Nominate somebody as chair.
4. A maximum of two people should answer each question that is asked.

CHAPTER 13

Mental Health: Not Just Surviving, But Thriving

To a metallurgist, stress and strain are scientific measures to describe the behaviour of a material when acted on by external forces. Under tension, a steel bar stretches and its diameter decreases. Up to a given load, the material will behave in a predictable way and return to its original shape when the load is removed. This is how springs work. However, every material has a 'yield point', where the load is such that it is permanently deformed and never returns to its original shape, and an 'ultimate strength', the point at which it breaks. It's easy to see why we now habitually use these words to describe the effects on ourselves of excessive workload.

At work, stress is a dirty word, but just as a sportsperson cannot avoid the inevitability of occasional defeat, it is futile to try to wholly remove stress from our careers. If we wish to progress or achieve any goal worthy of our efforts, then our objective should not be the removal of stress, but rather to manage it and to ensure that, like the steel bar, we are able to fully recover from its effects. If we do not, we too will eventually reach our yield point.

Understanding stress

Our careers develop in a competitive environment. As individuals, as teams and as organisations, we win and lose, move forward and sometimes back. Change, whether it be a new role, a new boss or a new job, can be full of opportunity, but also challenge; excitement and uncertainty; reward and risk. We cannot remove these from our career if we wish to progress. Indeed, not progressing arguably makes things worse – often people feel most stressed when most stuck.

It is in these high-pressure, high-stakes moments where we learn most about ourselves, where we have the greatest opportunity to progress most quickly, form great friendships and lifelong memories. But for every winner there is a loser. And sometimes that will be us. These low points are painful, but it is impossible to achieve greatness without experiencing failure along the way – and failure hurts, no matter who you are.

We do not have to enjoy these moments, but we have to accept their inevitability and, crucially, be able to recover from them.

We love hearing stories of redemption that begin with epic failure. They are exhilarating; the stuff of great stories and classic adventures. With the benefit of hindsight, such anecdotes can be amusing, inspiring and useful. But in the moment, when it's happening to us, they can be awful.

Are we more stressed than ever?

There is evidence that, for many people, feelings of work-related stress are increasing. A 2022 study by the American Psychological Association (APA) reported that American workers were experiencing year-on-year increases in stress and burnout. In their 'Work and Well-being Study', the APA found that 79 per cent of American workers had experienced work-related stress in the previous month, reporting a range of effects including lack of motivation, reduced energy, cognitive weariness and emotional exhaustion, while 44 per cent of those surveyed reported physical fatigue. Many of us will be familiar with the symptoms they list.

Furthermore, there is evidence that younger people report higher levels of stress than older generations. A 2023 report for the same organisation was apocalyptically headlined: 'Gen Z adults and young millennials are "completely overwhelmed" by stress'. Admittedly, the report and its respondents did not put the blame for this solely on work, but it is a sorry tale nevertheless.

There is an obvious caveat here. These studies were conducted around the time of the pandemic, a period of unprecedented uncertainty and anxiety for us all. However, there is little sign of this trend reversing. The results may have been accelerated by the upheaval of the pandemic, but did not begin with it, nor will its passing necessarily reverse them.

The nature of work itself is also changing at an unprecedented rate. The World Economic Forum's 'Future of Jobs Report' (2023) highlights continuing rapid shifts in how we work, where we work and what work will be like in the near future. It is by no means entirely pessimistic, but the rate of change it predicts in the workplace, change that will in some ways affect all of us, is astonishing.

Change brings us opportunity but also pressure, anxiety, uncertainty, a perception of reduced personal control over our situation and, therefore, increased levels of stress for many people. To highlight just two eye-popping data points from the WEF report:

- Employers anticipate a 23 per cent 'churn rate' of job roles (an amalgam measure of jobs emerging and jobs being eliminated) by 2028.

- 44 per cent of workers' skills will be disrupted by technology over the same period.

Because these numbers are averages, that means that in some sectors and roles, these rates will be very much higher. The WEF study looked at over 800 companies across forty-five countries, so it hides a wealth of more specific detail, but the trends are clear, dramatic, and span all industry sectors and economies.

If some stress is an everyday part of work, too much of it will eventually grind us down, unless we take care to mitigate it and recover. The World Health Organization defines burnout as being characterised by three dimensions:

1. Feelings of energy depletion or exhaustion; increased mental distance from one's job
2. Feelings of negativity or cynicism related to one's job
3. Reduced professional efficacy

Considering the above, it's clear that we can easily find ourselves in a vicious circle where excess levels of stress reduce our ability to function, thus increasing our levels of stress further.

Excessive stress affects our mental and our physical health. None of us possess natural immunity from its effects, but a stress overload is not an inevitability. It is important we understand the causes and symptoms of work-related stress and take measures to both mitigate their effects and recover properly. As we progress through our careers and find ourselves responsible for greater numbers of people, it is also important we are able to recognise the signs of burnout in others and are able, in turn, to help them.

Great jobs are stressful too

I hesitated before including a chapter detailing how work can be bad for our health. But these findings will not be new to you, and it would be disingenuous to pretend that pursuing a successful career is not difficult and demanding; people can burn out even doing jobs they love.

Stress and burnout are not specific to particular jobs nor to certain individuals. They can and do affect us all if we don't learn to manage, mitigate and reduce their effects. At the time of writing, two of the most famous and revered sportspeople in the UK, Ben Stokes (England men's cricket captain) and Owen Farrell (England men's rugby captain) have both recently taken long periods away from their sports, citing mental health issues.

A central premise of this book is that a good career is both rewarding and fulfilling. But we also know that it's not quite as simple as that. Poor jobs are bad for us but, unless we are careful, good ones can be too.

Causes of work-related stress

There are many reasons why we experience stress at work. If we wish to solve any problem, we must first understand what it is. To mitigate and recover from the effects of stress, we must first understand its source. The following are common contributors to work-related stress:

- Lack of job satisfaction
- Lack of time to complete critical tasks
- Lack of feedback – especially positive reinforcement

- Conflict
- Harassment
- Poor work–life balance
- Dirty (physically) or unsafe environment
- Threat of job-loss
- Change

One of the reasons that understanding leadership matters so much is because it teaches us how to think clearly about the problems we are faced with, understand the factors we can influence and take control of our circumstances. This is how we must approach the management of our stress levels throughout our careers.

One of the most debilitating causes of stress is the perception of powerlessness. Though we rarely have complete control over our circumstances through our careers, we are never powerless. Our sense of autonomy, as per Daniel Pink's definition, and the extent to which we are able to influence how, where and when we work, are both central to our ability to manage stress. We must understand this for ourselves – but as leaders we also have an important role in ensuring that those we are responsible for do the same.

Locus of control

In 1954, psychologist Julian B. Rotter developed the concept of 'locus of control'. In simple terms, he assessed people on the extent to which they believed that they were able to control the events in their life – it is important to note these are self-identified perceptions rather than objective statements of fact. Rotter described those with a strong sense of personal control as having an *internal* locus of control, and those who believed the events that influenced their lives were primarily driven by external factors, an *external* locus of control.

A person with an internal locus of control believes it is they who are in primary control of their life. This does not mean they feel in total control all the time, nor that they don't recognise that other forces play a role, but they believe that they are its primary motive force.

A person with an external locus of control believes factors that they cannot control, such as fate or luck, are life's primary drivers. For example, there is evidence that those who have a more internal locus of control are able to quit smoking more effectively than those who do not, believing it is they who control their behaviours, not the drug.

The primary purpose of this book is to give you the tools and confidence to take control over your career; to help you locate your 'career locus of control' within yourself.

Of course, external factors will always play a significant role in life, but with the right skills, focus and application, we can be the primary drivers of our career successes. We can take greater autonomy over how we work and thus work in ways that manage and mitigate our levels of stress effectively. Like sportspeople, sometimes we will get injured, sometimes others will out-perform us and sometimes we'll have off-days, but ultimately, it can be us who control our performance.

To ensure that stress and burnout do not weaken or overcome us, we must learn to recognise their symptoms, understand what tools are available to us to mitigate their effects and ensure we take the time and space to recover.

Autonomy, responsibility and consequence

Our mental health is a subject of great complexity that goes well beyond the scope of this book. However, it is possible to make some practical observations about how we understand and manage work-related stress.

Typically, stress is a function of three factors:

- Autonomy: The extent to which we are able to influence a particular outcome and control how we work to achieve it. Greater control over how we work reduces our levels of stress.
- Responsibility: The extent to which we are responsible for an outcome.
- Consequence: How significant the outcome is, whether for ourselves or for others.

The most straightforward way to understand how work can affect our levels of stress is to consider the interplay between these three factors. This interplay applies to everybody, irrespective of role, title, context or experience. Everybody finds situations of high responsibility, high consequence and low autonomy to be very stressful. This is typical of workplaces with poor cultures, and they are very stressful to work within.

If we are able to increase our autonomy, our stress will reduce, even if our responsibility and the consequences of our actions remain high. We should therefore consider the path towards greater autonomy as our primary route to stress reduction.

This is one reason why I believe that, contrary to popular belief, the most stressful jobs can be the most junior roles. In such roles, ambitious people especially find themselves facing a disparity between the extent to which they are able to control how they work (low) and their feeling of responsibility for the outcome (high). Conversely, as a global CEO, people would frequently say to me: 'I wouldn't fancy your job.' Sure, at times it was hard, but having done all the other jobs along the way, I knew with certainty that it was the best one on offer. A CEO has high responsibility, but also very high control if they're doing it right (which, to be fair, many don't, but that's for another book another day).

We have considered how understanding the principles of leadership enables us to take control of how we work, we have learned what to do if work isn't working for us and we have studied how to communicate more effectively, a critical component in shaping our working lives. These skills interlock and overlap, helping us find ways to master the events through our careers rather than be at their mercy. This does not stop stress from developing, but it both reduces its effects and helps us develop long-lasting habits for mitigation and recovery. We always have options, and the more options we feel we have, the less we feel the long-term effects of stress. The more boxed in we feel, the more stress can consume us.

For our careers to progress, we seek to increase our levels of responsibility and achieve promotion to roles where the consequences of our actions increase. However, this doesn't mean that stress must necessarily increase – as we become more senior, we should be able to exert greater control over how we work, and it is important we do in order to stay healthy.

We must find ways to strike a balance between the increased responsibility and consequence that promotion brings (and hence potentially increased levels of stress), and the opportunities it provides for greater self-direction and control over how we work (thus reducing our stress). When promoted, many people feel the effects of the former while failing to learn how to recognise and take advantage of the latter.

From day one of our careers, it is our ability to understand how to take greater control over how we work that will enable us to manage and moderate our stress levels, as well as help us to continually move forward towards our goals. Our mental and physical energy is a tank we can and must draw down from occasionally, but we must also take the time and care to ensure that it is regularly refilled.

If we don't, one day we will discover it dry.

Taking control over how we work

In a busy and successful career, we cannot wholly insulate ourselves from stress. But by recognising its causes and symptoms, we can learn how to recover from its effects.

Here are twelve practical steps you can take right now to bring your locus of control towards your own centre, increase your autonomy, and recover when the going gets tough.

1. Clarity: establish what matters most (and what doesn't)

The clearer you are about what success looks like for you, and what you need to focus on in order to help your team succeed, the better equipped you will be to prioritise tasks and cut clutter from your day. Work expands to fit the time available, so limit the time that you give it. Clarity allows you to focus on what matters most – and that is likely to cause you most stress if it's not done to the best of your ability.

2. Beware perfectionism

Good, we are often told, is the enemy of great. Sometimes this is both true and relevant. However, sometimes it's not. For much of what occupies our working days, 'great' can be the enemy of 'done'. Nothing is ever perfect. Things can always be done better, but doing something promptly and well is often more than enough. Perfect is unachievable and you should save striving for greatness for the projects and moments when it will count most.

Trade perfect for the satisfaction of a shortened to-do list.

3. Do the difficult or unpleasant jobs first

All jobs involve doing some things that we don't enjoy. However, some of these tasks are also very important. It is tempting to put them off by occupying our time with things we enjoy, or displacement activities where we fool ourselves into believing that we're busy.

The consequence of such postponements is unnecessary and self-imposed stress. Avoidance and prevarication are a common cause of sleepless nights and anxiety, yet the solution is entirely within our control. De-stress by putting urgent or unwelcome tasks at the top of your to-do list every day, and make them the first thing you do. Or set aside a specific regular time of each week to do them.

4. Quit multitasking

We have already covered in some detail the importance of using our time well.

A primary reason for stress and burnout is over-work. One of the most effective ways to avoid this is to become better at managing our time by devoting as much as possible to what matters most and by clearing clutter from our diaries. Re-invest some of the time you get back in yourself.

Multitasking is simply the worst of many habits that destroy our productivity. We flit from task to task, put off the things we don't want to do, allow ourselves to be distracted by social media, our inboxes and colleagues. It is easy to convince ourselves that we have been busy while achieving very little. If necessary, revisit Chapter 5 and familiarise yourself with the methods discussed there in order to increase the quality of your outputs while reducing time wastage on low-priority filler.

Set yourself a time limit to complete priority tasks and give greater structure to how you work by scheduling breaks every hour. Signal to co-workers that you do not wish to be disturbed by wearing headphones or by finding a quiet place away from your desk (and your emails, if possible) to work. Switch your phone to 'do not disturb' mode to ensure you receive no notifications to distract you while you are concentrating.

Structuring your workday around focusing on the tasks that are really going to make a difference, and cutting as many as you can of those that don't, enhances productivity and your personal ROI. And it makes you feel more in control.

5. Take control of your day

Perhaps the most potent everyday reminder of how little control we have over our working time is our diary. People can often add us to meetings without our permission – sometimes without even telling us. We see our diaries clog up and despair.

Think about who you would like to be able to see your diary and who can (and cannot) add meetings to it. If it is in your power to edit these permissions, then do so. Do not simply sleepwalk through your week.

We all need to be able to say no to more meetings. If you feel you lack the authority to do so alone, ask your boss this question:

> Can you help me take greater control over my working day so I can focus on the areas we have both agreed matter most?

Even a 10 per cent reduction in the number of meetings you are obliged to attend would make a significant difference to your week.

Remember, increased control means decreased stress.

6. Work-based recovery

Take regular breaks throughout the day to recharge. Physical activity, even a short walk, can help release tension and improve your mood. Go outside. Make phone calls from a bench in the park rather than from your desk. Get some natural light and fresh air. Many workplaces provide opportunities and spaces for people to recharge through the day. Make use of them; they are there for a reason.

After more than an hour sitting in the same place focusing on the same task, our productivity rapidly declines. Remember, being busy is not the same as being productive. Take a break. Get up, go for a walk, get a coffee, have a chat. Think about something else.

Take a lunch break and avoid eating at your desk if possible. Sitting in the same place, scrolling through social media, will not help. Movement is beneficial for both your physical and mental well-being. Not only does it help you recharge, but you'd be surprised by how many new ideas and perspectives pop into your mind when you give it a chance to relax or just think about something new.

7. Invest time in yourself

In my first book, *No Bullsh*t Leadership*, I compared each of us to the counters we find in the board game Trivial Pursuit. To win the game, we must fill our counter with one each of six differently coloured segments. These segments represent the various aspects of our lives: work, family, friends, hobbies, passions, and so on. To stay healthy and happy, we must find a balance that allows us to take care of all these different aspects of what makes us *us*. It's easy to wake up one day and realise that work has consumed all else. If we allow that to happen, it is very difficult to then find outlets to manage our stress, recharge and recover.

Recovery is very personal – it means different things to different people. We don't always need inactivity in order to recharge; sometimes activity is more effective. Indeed, though we all need a couple of hours on the sofa watching crappy TV from time to time, if we end up ruminating, doom-scrolling and checking emails, it may end up making us feel worse. For you, recovery might mean sky-diving, or camping with the kids, or five-a-side football, or writing, or stamp collecting, or dancing, or clubbing.

Whatever it is, make sure you're on your to-do list. Recovery is not simply 'not work'; it's an active investment in the other aspects of your life.

8. One selfish hour every week

It is common, especially for parents of young children, to get to the end of the week never having had a moment that is wholly and solely theirs. It's exhausting.

Find an activity that you do at least once a week that is totally and completely selfish, that allows no space in your brain for anything else. Everybody can find an hour – and once you have, fill it with an activity that allows no space for anything else to intrude. If you spend it just staring into space, you might physically rest, but your brain will rapidly retake control, reminding you of all the things you should be doing. Before you know it, you'll be up and replying to emails.

Instead, find an activity that is fully consuming and that allows no space for anything else. For me, it's tennis. No matter how stressed I am – no matter what else is happening in my life or in the world – for those ninety minutes, it is impossible for anything else to intrude. It is utterly refreshing.

Find yours and try it. It works.

9. Firebreaks

There are advantages to hybrid working, but there is also evidence that it increases work-related stress because it makes it more difficult to set boundaries between work and everything else that matters in your life. If you don't create spaces, physical and mental, where work cannot intrude, then it becomes very difficult to recharge and recover. To avoid this, build firewalls to protect your lifc outside of work.

You should establish clear boundaries between your work and personal lives. Avoid checking work emails during non-working hours and communicate your availability (and unavailability) to colleagues. This is more acceptable now than ever before. Sometimes long hours are an inevitable part of a successful career, but they should not unthinkingly become the norm. Creating a balance between work and personal life is crucial for preventing burnout.

10. Healthy habits

There are specific techniques you can use to prevent and manage stress. Practices such as meditation, exercise, yoga or progressive muscle relaxation can help manage stress and enhance focus.

Remember that everyone's experience of stress is different, and it may require a combination of strategies to find what works best for you. Finding the right one may be a process of trial and error, but won't be wasted time. Regularly reassess how you manage your stress, your boundaries and how you recover, and adjust as needed to maintain a healthy and balanced work life.

You shouldn't see this process as offsetting, but rather as an integral and indispensable part of how you develop a long, successful and healthy career. Many employers run programmes to help manage stress, both in and out of work. Talk to your boss or the HR department to find out what's available in your company. If nothing exists, suggest setting some up – I guarantee there'll be a good uptake.

Increasing numbers of people are forced to take time out from work, sometimes for long periods, because of the effects of stress. A conscious plan of your own will help you to protect yourself, but you should also remind your employer, if necessary, that a modest and smart investment in helping others do the same is enlightened self-interest.

No plan is ever perfect, but you must keep yourself on your to-do list and recognise that the best way to ensure you have the energy and enthusiasm to fulfil your career ambitions is to regularly carve out time to recover. It's easy to allow your recovery time to gradually drift to the bottom of your priority list, but people won't remember the days when you worked shorter hours, or switched your notifications off, or took a longer lunch break. But they will most certainly remember if you're the person who always brings the energy and the focus, every time it's needed most.

11. Remember everybody else

For the majority of your career, you will have people you are responsible for. These people want the same as you. They too want a great career and to reduce their stress levels. The best way for them to do that is to have a boss who understands and does the same.

If you want to run a team that thrives, re-read these rules and help those who work for you implement them. Ensure you are actively talking to those you are responsible for about how they can increase their autonomy, reduce their stress levels and improve their recovery. Just the simple act of having the conversation might be transformational for some.

12. Always wear sunscreen

And always use all of your holiday allowance.

We all get stressed, but we need not become overwhelmed

Modern life is stressful and modern work is stressful. It is disingenuous to pretend otherwise. However, it's not inevitable that you become overwhelmed. You should not be surprised to experience stress, but you must learn to understand its causes, recognise its symptoms, and implement the ways through which you can increase your level of control and recover properly from it. In the end, it is a very personal process that others can help with, but you must find what works for you.

Awareness of mental health is greater than it has ever been, as is a wider understanding of the causes and effects of work-related stress. Things may not be perfect, but they are better than they were, meaning that there are a growing number of programmes in place to help across more and more companies. If such support structures exist where you work, make the most of them. If they don't, challenge your employers to re-think.

Most important of all, don't be afraid to ask for help. This may mean a conversation with your boss, a mentor, a colleague or a member of the HR team. As with all important conversations, once you've started it, you may be pleasantly surprised at the direction it takes. If you can, bring solutions with you – not least because it will make it easier for them to help you.

Don't leave it until it is too late.

Nobody is immune to the effects of too much stress – even

doing jobs we love. If we wish to have long and successful careers, we must learn to drag our locus of control towards our centre and to protect our recovery periods. And to do the same for those who work for us.

Ten practical steps for a happier and more fulfilled life

You're not a machine, and you can't run on all cylinders indefinitely. The key isn't balance in the traditional sense; it's alignment. Success comes not from grinding nonstop but from balancing effort with restoration. When you care for your body, mind and spirit, you're not only more effective – you're more fulfilled.

1. Define what success means for you

Success isn't a universal formula – it's personal. Decide what matters most to you at any given point – this may change over time: career milestones, relationships, family health, or creative pursuits.

Be intentional about your priorities and don't let societal expectations hijack your goals. Once you know what matters to you, you can allocate your time and energy accordingly.

2. Boundaries

Set and enforce clear boundaries at work and in your personal life. Whether it's defining 'no work' hours or learning to be better at saying no to commitments that don't align with your priorities or values.

Your time is a zero-sum game: every yes is a no to something else. Choose wisely.

Boundaries protect your time and mental energy.

3. View stress as a signal, not an enemy

Stress isn't inherently bad – it's your body's way of saying something needs attention. Ask yourself: is this stress coming from poor planning, overcommitment, or a fear I need to face?

Use stress as a guide to problem-solve, delegate, or adjust your expectations.

Avoid numbing it; instead, tackle the root cause.

4. Recovery is non-negotiable

Sleep, downtime and active rest (like walks, yoga or hobbies) are where your brain consolidates ideas and your body resets. Rest is a cornerstone of productivity.

Protect your sleep. Aim for seven to eight hours, and create an evening routine that signals when you should be winding down. Whenever possible, try to go to bed at the same time each night.

5. Work smarter, not just harder

Hard work is essential, but without focus and a sense of progress leads to burnout. Dedicate your energy to the tasks that matter most and that will give you the highest return. Learn to become an effective delegator. Remember: 80 per cent of your results are likely to come from 20 per cent of your effort – so make that time count. Double down on what moves the needle.

6. Stay physically active

Movement is medicine – so find what works for you. Whether it's strength training, yoga, tennis or a thirty-minute brisk dog-walk, regular exercise improves your mood, focus and resilience to stress. And it makes you feel a whole lot better about yourself.

Exercise doesn't have to be extreme; it's consistency that counts. Make it part of your daily rhythm, like brushing your teeth.

7. Fuel your body for energy, not just convenience

What we eat and drink matters enormously to how we feel and our levels of energy. Great nutrition is mostly common sense and isn't about perfection – it's about making small, sustainable choices.

Eat a balanced plate of proteins, carbohydrates and vegetables. Limit sugar, processed foods and sugary drinks. Drink plenty of water through the day and limit caffeine in the afternoon to avoid wrecking your sleep.

8. Audit your relationships and social circle

The people you surround yourself with matter to your mental state and levels of energy.

Spend time with those who lift you up, make you laugh and inspire you, not those who drain or criticise.

Deep, meaningful connections protect against stress and loneliness, but strong relationships don't just happen; you need to find time for them and make sure you nurture them.

9. Create space for joy and play

It's not all about productivity – joy matters. Spend time on activities that have no goal other than to make you happy, whether that's painting, cooking, playing music, or exploring the outdoors. These moments of play refresh your perspective and keep life joyful.

Always have something in your diary that you're looking forward to – even if it's as simple as dinner with a friend.

10. Regularly reflect and adjust course

Periodically, take stock – don't just drift.

Are you still clear on your goals, have they evolved and are you focusing on the right things in order to achieve them? Are you managing stress in a healthy way – sometimes we all get into bad habits.

Reflection helps you find solutions before burnout or dissatisfaction creep in. Make sure you are always on your to-do list.

Chris Hirst's Golden Rules

1. Attitude beats aptitude.
2. Everything is difficult until it becomes easy.
3. Know what your boss needs from you and make it your focus.
4. The squeaky wheel gets the oil – so squeak away.
5. You can't be someone else, but you can get out of your own way.
6. Failure isn't an occupational hazard; it is a prerequisite for success.
7. Nobody cares about your career as much as you.
8. Leadership is difficult, but not complicated.
9. Nearly all success (at work) comes down to preparation and practice.
10. Be world class at the things that require no talent.
11. Prioritising is having the courage to cut.

12. When you bring someone a problem, always have a proposed solution in mind.

13. Being busy is not the same as being effective.

14. Talent is an excuse we use to explain the performance of others.

15. Leadership Impact = Clarity × Action.

16. Competence will suffice 95 per cent of the time.

17. Fifty per cent of effective communication is listening.

18. What one thing can I cut today?

19. Make sure you are on your to-do list, and somewhere near the top.

20. Understanding is a prelude to solving.

21. Quit multi-tasking.

22. Recovery is not simply 'not work'; it is active investment in you.

23. You are not a zero-sum game.

Conclusion

A successful career is more art than science. It's a scattered collage of events from which, with the right guidance and application, you can build the picture you want. All careers have their share of ups and downs, but some people find great fulfilment and success in spite of them.

The essence of a successful career is progress; we wish to increase our level of responsibility, our sense of reward (emotional and physical) and our autonomy. The greater the control we achieve over how we work, our direction and ultimately our career itself, the more fulfilled we will feel.

However, growing numbers of people around the world have become disillusioned with work, employment and careers because they experience the opposite: a disconnect between the effort they put in and the return they receive. Like a balloon inflating inside a closed box, the walls hem them in. They work harder and harder, and see others do the same, but do not progress. And can see no way to do so. At best they quiet-quit, at worst burn out. It is in everybody's interests that this problem is solved.

Successful societies are based on realistic aspiration – that those who work hard get a fair return for their efforts; that progress based on merit is possible for all if they are diligent, resilient, prepared to learn and are good team-mates. I am often told on social media that meritocracy is a myth, but this is only true if we allow it to be so. The most successful societies and the most successful companies are places where people believe progress is possible for them and can see others like them who have achieved just that. It is no coincidence that these are the organisations that grow and create yet more opportunity.

My ambition has been to show you that when it comes to your career you do have agency, and to give you the knowledge, support and foundational skills to make the most of it. Of course, the vagaries of fortune will always be waiting to trip you – errors, wrong turns, bad actors and any number of trials are inevitable. Success demands not that you ignore these (sometimes that's almost impossible) but understand that there are always things you can control and do.

Mistakes are only fatal if we keep making the same ones.

You are not a zero-sum game. You can grow, change and achieve the remarkable, but it's just that bit easier with a little help. The more valuable you become to your employer, your clients or your customers, the less dependent you are on the whims and ways of others and the greater your ability to control your future direction.

Career success depends primarily on our ability to collaborate effectively with other equally imperfect people, all of whom are also pursuing their own goals. It is not the functional aspects of our job that accelerate us forward (or hold us back) but our ability to form effective relationships with the people around us. This simple truth is so often neither understood nor explained. It is our attitude rather than our aptitude that primarily determines our career success. Indeed, it is attitude that drives aptitude.

The most powerful career skill anyone can develop is to be the person who everybody wants on their team; the person who warms a room when they walk in, who finds solutions rather than problems, who offers support rather than criticism. This requires no talent, but if that sounds flippant then you haven't been paying attention. Such people are also those who learn most quickly, who adapt most effectively and who get shit done. They are the people who get promoted first, get the pay rises and fulfil their personal ambitions; the people who become indispensable.

Ultimately, nobody cares as much about your career as you. Not least because they've all got their own shit to deal with. This book has shown you how you take control over yours by focusing your energies and efforts in the right places, and given you the tools and confidence to get what you really want. By understanding these basic building blocks and principles, those that determine all successful careers, you too can make work work for you.

Nothing contained within these pages is beyond you. You can do it all – and if you do, then you will thrive anywhere. Which means that a great and rewarding career is within your grasp.

Index